Welcome to the Peace of Mind Community!

Stay Informed
Peace of Mind's website and monthly newsletter offer practices you can use in the classroom and updates about events, training and resources. Visit our website and join our mailing list to keep up to date.

Get Support
If you are new to us, consider taking our 2-hour online course "Getting Started with Peace of Mind." For the link, visit the "Educators" section on our website.

Prepare to Teach
Find the materials you need for this curriculum in the "Shop" section of our website.

TeachPeaceofMind.org

Questions? Comments?
We'd love to hear from you!
info@TeachPeaceofMind.org

Peace of Mind Core Curriculum for Early Childhood
Peace of Mind Core Curriculum for First and Second Grade
Peace of Mind Core Curriculum for Third to Fifth Grade
Peace of Mind Curriculum for Fourth and Fifth Grade

TeachPeaceofMind.org

Peace of Mind Inc., Washington, D.C.
https://TeachPeaceofMind.org
Copyright 2019
ISBN 978-0-9976954-6-5
LCCN 2019909785

Peace of Mind is a trademark of Peace of Mind Inc. All rights reserved. No part of this curriculum may be reproduced, stored in a retrieval system, or transmitted by any means, electronic or otherwise, without prior written permission from Peace of Mind Inc. Please contact Peace of Mind, Inc. via TeachPeaceofMind.org to request permission.

Cover and interior design: Schwa Design Group
Logo: Pittny Creative

Published 2019

Support for *Peace of Mind*

I use Peace of Mind every day in my classroom not only because it supports my own personal meditation practice, but also because I have seen the positive impact it has had on my students over the past six years. Peace of Mind should be in every classroom in America because every child will benefit from looking inward, understanding themselves, and sharing their positivity with others.
- **Jared Catapano, 4th Grade Teacher, Washington D.C.**

I started using the curriculum and it's wonderful! The lessons are easy to follow and very well thought out. The curriculum fits well with the Mindful Schools training that I did a few years ago. I'm very pleased with my purchase.
- **Kree Barus, Grade 2 Learning Support Teacher, American School, Jeddah S.A.**

This is an extraordinary curriculum, at once practical and visionary. The lessons are thoughtfully and meticulously scaffolded as the children are guided step-by-step into an understanding of how their brains work, how to interact with the world with kindness, and how to master themselves. In this age of anxiety, what could be more important or valuable than to teach children at an early age how to interpret and navigate their big emotions, calm themselves, and by extension, each other?
- **Val Carroll, Arts Integration Educator, Washington D.C.**

We want our children to master their academics but we equally want them to master being good citizens who care about one another and the world at large. The Peace [of Mind] Program does just that. In an age where bullying has become a major problem, the Program is proactive instead of reactive, thereby eliminating some of those problems before they begin.
- **Jackie Snowden, former Assistant Principal, Washington D.C.**

The importance of teaching kindness, compassion, how to get along, what to do if there is bullying, and how to handle or possibly to avoid conflicts cannot be overstated. The Peace [of Mind] program works. We have been able to see the difference between the students' ability to handle conflicts over the years and we have seen improvement.
- **Lisa Jensen and Blake Yedwab, Elementary School Teachers, Washington D.C.**

Henry and Friends Storybook Series

These delightful, captivating books are full of powerful practical methods for kids - and their parents.
    - **Rick Hanson, Ph.D.,** author of *Resilient, Hardwiring Happiness,* and *Buddha's Brain*

About Tyaja Uses the THiNK Test
In this simple and clear story, Linda Ryden offers valuable lessons for our children to bring more clarity, care and thoughtfulness to the power of words.
    - **Oren Jay Sofer,** author of *Say What You Mean: A Mindful Approach to Nonviolent Communication*

About Henry is Kind
Linda Ryden's kids' book about Heartfulness practice is bright, fun and engaging, which is wonderful because it means kids will love it. And, the book provides an easy way for teachers and parents to help children understand and enjoy being kind, which means adults will love it too. It is a pleasure to think of the benefits Henry is Kind may bring to children and families.
    - **Sharon Salzberg,** author of *Real Happiness* and *Real Love*

About Sergio Sees the Good
I absolutely adore Sergio. It's a really relatable story for both kids and adults. The science is just right - totally accessible but not "dumbed down." I love the part about the cactus because you show that it's not all bad to focus on the negative stuff and there's a logical reason why evolution didn't do away with it. I think it's also great that you touched on how one can overcome the negativity bias in daily life by noticing and feeling grateful for the "little, good things", even though that feels more effortful.
    - **Dr. Elizabeth Hoffman,** Neuroscientist

About Rosie's Brain
This wonderful gem of a book helped my son understand how his brain works. The day he came home from school, having had difficulty keeping his hands to himself, we read this book together. He's been talking ever since about how he needs to let his pre-frontal cortex control his actions and not his amygdala (Amy). The illustrations are so sweet.
    - **Petrina Hollingsworth,** parent

Contents

I. Introduction	1
II. Overview	3
III. Lessons At-A-Glance	10
IV. Preparing to Teach 4th and 5th Graders	14
V. Lessons	
Unit 1 Welcome to Peace Class	17
Week 1: Welcome to Peace Class	18
Week 2: Favorite Things	25
Week 3: What Works for You?	28
Week 4: See, Hear, Feel	33
Unit 2 Learning our Body's Language	37
Week 5: Flashlight Body Scan	38
Week 6: Finding Your Feelings	42
Week 7: Finding Your Feelings Story	48
Unit 3 Empathy in Action	53
Week 8: Heartfulness	54
Week 9: The THiNK Test	59
Week 10: Putting the THiNK Test to Work	64
* **Note** *Talking about Bullying*	*68*
Week 11: Getting Bullied	70
Week 12: The Role of a Bystander	74
Week 13: Understanding Bullying Behavior	78
Unit 4 Gratitude and the Negativity Bias	83
Week 14: Hacking your Brain: The Negativity Bias and Gratitude	84
Week 15: Sergio's Scales	89
Week 16: Gratitude Cards	94
Unit 5 Brain Science and Mindfulness	97
Week 17: Rosie's Brain	98
Week 18: Brain Review	102
Week 19: Your Brain and Basketball	109

Unit 6 Conflict Resolution — 113
- Week 20: Conflict Escalator Review: Swings are for Babies — 114
- Week 21: MOFL: Apology Practice — 119
- Week 22: Conflict Toolbox Matching Game — 124
- Week 23: Conflict C.A.T. Role Play — 129
- Week 24: Create Your Own Scenarios — 133
- Week 25: The Conflict C.A.T. Game — 136

Unit 7 The Story I'm Telling Myself — 141
- Week 26: Remote Control Mindfulness — 142
- Week 27: Where are My Thoughts? — 146
- Week 28: Fast and Slow Thinking — 151
- Week 29: Don't Believe Everything You Think — 155
- Week 30: Gender Stereotypes — 162
- Week 31: Standing up for Others — 166

Unit 8 Closing out the Year — 171
- Week 32: The Kindest Things — 172
- Week 33: Capstone Project — 176

VI. Materials for Lessons — 179
- Skits — 180
- Worksheets and Posters — 194
- Books, Videos and Games — 211

VII. Resources — 213
- Comprehensive Whole School Integration — 214
- Home-School Connection — 216
- Teacher Support — 217

VIII. Bibliography — 220

IX. Credits — 222

X. Appreciation — 223
- About the authors — 225

I. Introduction

Welcome to the *Peace of Mind Curriculum for Grades 4 and 5*! Since we published the *Peace of Mind Core Curriculum for Grades 3-5*, our field has evolved and we have continued to learn new things about how to deliver this work to older elementary students. Our desire to share what we have learned and requests from educators for more material inspired us to write this curriculum.

We have written The *Peace of Mind Curriculum for Grades 4 and 5* as both an introduction and a continuation. If your fourth and fifth grade students are new to *Peace of Mind*, this curriculum is for you. If your students have had the *Peace of Mind Core Curriculum for Grades 3-5* for one or two years, this will work for you too; you'll find notes throughout linking this curriculum to that one.

This curriculum includes engaging lessons that integrate mindfulness practices and brain science as the foundation for teaching social and emotional learning and conflict resolution. Relative to the *Peace of Mind Core Curriculum for Grades 3-5*, you will find more movement and pair-sharing. You will also find new, age-appropriate lessons relating to the embodiment of feelings, bullying, standing up for others, gratitude and the negativity bias, stereotypes and bias, and solving conflicts accompanied by new storybooks, skits and videos.

This curriculum, like our first three, is the result of what we have learned works for real children in the dynamic setting of a public school classroom here in Washington D.C. We offer this humbly, as we know that your classroom and school will have their own unique needs and goals. We hope that you will bring your own experience and skills to bear in adapting the lessons to meet your students' needs in the best way possible.

What *Peace of Mind* offers is more than simply mindfulness practice or social and emotional skills: we offer an integrated, weekly, year-after-year program that teaches skills for life. Combined with your passion and dedication as a teacher, this is a very powerful, transformative combination for our children.

If you find value in teaching *Peace of Mind*, we hope you will share it with your colleagues and friends. Our nonprofit organization, Peace of Mind Inc, exists to be of service to educators who want to bring mindfulness, kindness and conflict resolution to their students. Please help us spread the word!

Thank you for taking up this important work. Your community and your students need what you have to give.

In peace,   Linda and Cheryl

Curriculum Overview

Welcome to **the *Peace of Mind Curriculum for Grades 4 and 5*!** All of the ***Peace of Mind Curricula,*** including this one, integrate mindfulness practice, brain science, social emotional learning, and conflict resolution for elementary school students.

In this curriculum we have also included lessons on recognizing and addressing implicit bias, noticing and responding to gender stereotypes, and understanding and standing up to bullying behavior.

The **Peace of Mind Program** helps students develop the skills to notice and manage their emotions, to focus their attention, to practice kindness, empathy and gratitude, to build healthy relationships, and to solve conflicts peacefully.

Peace of Mind also aims to equip and inspire kids to address unkindness and unfairness when they encounter it at school or with friends, and to feel confident in their capacities to contribute to making the world a better place.

Teaching the ***Peace of Mind Curriculum*** weekly over the course of the whole school year, year after year, and integrating elements of ***Peace of Mind*** into every day, creates positive change in a classroom and, over time, in school climate, moving schools toward kindness and inclusion.

For an overview of the philosophy, history and goals of the **Peace of Mind Program**, please watch the short video introduction by Peace Teacher and curriculum author Linda Ryden on our website: TeachPeaceofMind.org/videos/.

Curriculum Structure

All ***Peace of Mind*** curricula include three critical, integrated components:

- Mindfulness
- Brain Science
- Social and Emotional Learning (SEL) with an emphasis on Kindness, Conflict Resolution. This curriculum includes a focus on and addressing bias and stereotypes, as well.

Every lesson begins with mindfulness practice, and every lesson ends with Kindness Pal practice. Brain science, social emotional learning (SEL) and conflict resolution lessons are particularly effective because they are built upon this foundation.

Mindfulness is the practice of paying attention to our thoughts, our feelings, and what is happening around us, and putting some space between our reactions and our response. Mindfulness practice in this curriculum might include quietly sitting to focus on breath awareness, practicing mindful listening, noticing how our bodies feel when we have different emotions, engaging in active movement, and more.

Mindfulness practice is becoming more prevalent in schools because research shows that mindfulness training can help to enhance children's attention and focus (Zenner et al., 2014; Zoogman et al. 2015), improve self-control and emotion regulation (Metz et al., 2013), and improve overall social emotional competence including increased empathy, perspective-taking, and emotional control, and less peer-rated aggression (Schonert-Reichl et al., 2014; Schonert-Reichl & Lawlor, 2010).

Social and Emotional Learning (SEL) is the process through which we learn to manage emotions; set and achieve positive goals; feel and show empathy for others; establish and manage positive relationships; and make responsible decisions. *(CASEL.org)*

A growing body of research shows that tending to students' social and emotional needs has positive benefits. A meta-analysis of 213 school-based SEL programs with over 270,000 students found that students who received SEL instruction, compared to a control group, showed significantly improved social and emotional skills, attitudes and behavior, and an 11 percent gain in academic achievement. (Durlak et al., 2011).

Peace of Mind's SEL components include kindness practice in every lesson through Kindness Pals; lessons on empathy, gratitude practice, building connection, addressing bullying, implicit bias, apologizing and using a set of tools to resolve conflicts peacefully.

Ultimately, the goal of ***Peace of Mind*** is to create a school culture of kindness. Creating a kinder, more positive school climate and dedicating class time for social and emotional learning are two important and evidence-based approaches to bullying prevention (Bradshaw, 2015; O'Brennan & Bradshaw, 2013).

Peace of Mind's goals and lesson structure are aligned with the 5 Core Competencies identified by the Collaborative for Social and Emotional Learning (CASEL).

Peace of Mind teaches Mindfulness-based Social and Emotional Learning.
We know that mindfulness and SEL both have positive benefits for our students and our schools. But here's what's really exciting: we have learned in over a decade of teaching this work to students that integrating mindfulness with SEL is an even more transformative approach than teaching either mindfulness or SEL on its own.

> *Ultimately, when taught and learned together, mindfulness and SEL have the potential to transform our communities and our world with the former cultivating the tendencies for compassion and ethical ways of living and the latter teaching the skills to make that happen.*
>
> - Linda Lantieri, Senior Program Advisor for CASEL and Adjunct Assistant Professor, Columbia University, Teachers College

Brain science is a key ingredient in **Peace of Mind**'s mindfulness-based SEL approach. **Peace of Mind** offers students a basic understanding of the roles of the amygdala, the hippocampus and the prefrontal cortex in reacting and responding to stimuli. This knowledge helps kids understand how and why we get angry, for example, and how and why practicing mindfulness can help us calm down enough to make a decision that moves us closer to the outcome we'd like to have.

We can't know what challenges our children will face as they grow, but we have confidence that the combination of these internal and external approaches will give students the ability to meet them with skill and kindness.

Now let's have a look at the curriculum.

Lesson Themes

The 33 weekly lessons in the *Peace of Mind Curriculum for 4th and 5th Grade* are divided into 7 units focused in the following areas:

Unit 1: Welcome (back) to Peace Class
The first four lessons introduce some new and some familiar mindfulness practices (for those who have had *Peace of Mind* before), encouraging students to take ownership of their practice this year, learning to notice which practices are most helpful to them.

Unit 2: Learning our Body's Language
In this unit, we explore the embodiment of feelings. When we can notice where feelings begin in our bodies, it gives us a head start on gaining control over how we respond to them.

Unit 3: Empathy in Action
In this unit, we'll review Heartfulness and the THiNK Test and then move into a set of lessons on perspective taking related to understanding and addressing bullying.

Unit 4: Gratitude and the Negativity Bias
In this unit, we explore our brain's tendency to focus on the negative and how we can balance this tendency with gratitude practice.

Unit 5: Brain Science and Mindfulness
In this unit, we review the functions and interrelatedness of three key parts of our brains: the amygdala, the hippocampus and the prefrontal cortex. We put this knowledge to work in a new skit.

Unit 6: Conflict Resolution
In this unit, we integrate everything we've done until this point. Through discussion, skits and games, we apply what we've been learning about mindfulness, kindness, empathy, and brain science to the challenge of resolving conflicts peacefully.

Unit 7: The Story I'm Telling Myself
In this unit, we address the most challenging topics in our curriculum: noticing our own thoughts and learning about stereotypes and implicit bias. In this unit we are helping children begin to use the mindfulness and other skills they've been learning to understand and respond to societal challenges.

End of Year
We close the year with the Kindness Things exercise and a student-directed Capstone Project that invites students to reflect on how they will put what they have learned this year to work.

Lesson Sequence

Lessons are designed to be taught in the order in which they are presented. However, we know that in some cases, it may make sense to you to change the order of lessons to meet your students' needs or to coincide with events in your school community. Please do what you think best meets the needs of your class.

The very first lesson you teach about mindfulness is actually the first step toward peaceful conflict resolution in your classroom. From Week 1, you will be building the foundation that will enable children to solve conflicts with empathy, compassion and skill. Every lesson is a critical piece of the foundation for successful conflict resolution. Without the foundation, the conflict resolution lessons themselves will be less effective.

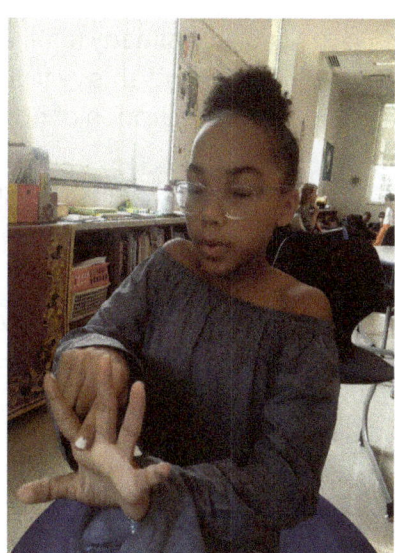

However, if you are seeing a great deal of conflict among your students in the beginning of the year, and would like to get to those lessons more quickly, here is an alternative sequence: Teach all of Unit 1 and then go directly to Unit 5, Brain Science and then to Unit 6, Conflict Resolution. After Unit 6, you return to Units 2, 3 and 4, and then move to Unit 7.

All of the lessons bear repeating. If you feel your class needs more practice in a certain area, feel free to repeat a lesson, or segment of the lesson, that feels helpful.

Lesson Framework

Each lesson includes the following components:

- **Mindfulness and Mindfulness Helper**
  Mindfulness is the foundation for everything we teach. Reinforcing each child's ability to be a Mindfulness Helper is important. Helping to the lead the class in mindfulness practice supports each child in making the practices their own. Leadership of this part of class may be particularly beneficial for children who do not have leadership opportunities in other areas of their lives.

- **Lesson**
  Weekly lessons are designed to be engaging and fun with a balance of listening, discussion and activity. Some lessons focus primarily on introducing a new mindfulness practice; most start with a mindfulness practice as the foundation for topics described above.

- **Storybooks and Skits**
  Six lessons use topical storybooks to help engage kids in the ideas and

skills being taught. Other lessons engage students in skits to help them practice using the skills and tools they are learning, so that they are available to them when they are really needed!

- **Kindness Pals**
  All lessons close with Kindness Pals (except Weeks 32 and 33). Not only do Kindness Pals give students a way to practice kindness, they are an essential tool for building a positive and inclusive classroom and school community.

  If you are already familiar with Kindness Pals, you'll find a few new components this year. If you are new to this, or need a reminder, you will find a description of how Kindness Pals work in the lesson for Week 1.

  The Kindness Pal practice at the end of each lesson may include:

  - Sharing what pals did for each other in the previous week.
  - Assignment of new Kindness Pals.
  - The Kindness Pal Challenge: a new activity that invites students to find out as much as they can about each other in 90 seconds.
  - Sharing what pals learned during the Challenge.

  You may not have time for all of these components in every class. That's fine. You might choose to integrate the Kindness Pal Challenge at another time during the week.

  > *NOTE: In some lessons, you'll find guidance to assign your new Kindness Pals before the end of class in order to have new pals work together on pair activities.*

Materials Needed

You will need the following materials on hand for this curriculum:

- a bell or a chime;
- a means to show videos to your class;
- a talking object, such as a small stuffed animal or bean bag;
- six readily-available storybooks.
  - *Weird, Dare and Tough* by Erin Frankel
  - *Rosie's Brain, Sergio Sees the Good, and Tyaja Uses the THiNK Test* by Linda Ryden

Optional: You may also be interested in investing in these classroom resources. They are not required, but all support the lessons you will be teaching:

- *Ways to Practice Mindfulness - Classroom Poster* that reminds kids of the practices they've learned, and helps them to choose a practice of their own as needed.
- *Peace of Mind Anchor Charts* for the Brain and Conflict Toolbox.
- *The Conflict CAT Game* used in the Conflict Resolution section.
- *Brainy the Puppet*, to help illustrate the Hand Model of the Brain

Please visit TeachPeaceofMind.org/shop/ for a full range of classroom resources.

Teacher Guidance

The first paragraph of each lesson offers you an overview of the lesson.

All of the lessons offer suggested scripts for you. They are there if you need them. Please use them as a support, but feel free to teach the lesson in your own words in the way that feels most natural to you.

Still have questions?

After reading the introductory material here, you may still feel that you would like some support preparing to teach *Peace of Mind*.

We have created a two-hour online course just for you called "**Getting Started with Peace of Mind.**" You can find a link to the course in the Educators section of our website: TeachPeaceofMind.org.

Lessons At-a-Glance

Unit 1 – Welcome to Peace Class			
Week	Mindfulness Skill	Lesson Objective(s)	CASEL Competencies*
1. Welcome to Peace Class	Take 5 Breathing	Review the concept of mindfulness and re-establish the foundation for mindfulness practice. Launch Kindness Pals for the year.	2, 3, 4
2. My Kindness Pal's Favorite Thing	Take 5 Breathing	Learn a new way of practicing mindfulness. Practice kindness.	1, 2, 3, 4
3. What Works for You?	Gravity Hands, 4 Square Breathing, and Clench and Release	Notice how your body responds to different practices and what is most helpful to you. Practice kindness.	1, 2, 3, 4, 5
4. See, Hear, Feel	See Hear Feel	Learn a new way of practicing mindfulness. Practice kindness.	1, 2, 3, 4,

Unit 2 – Learning our Body's Language			
Week	Mindfulness Skill	Lesson Objective(s)	CASEL Competencies*
5. Flashlight Body Scan	Flashlight Body Scan	Learn that we can be aware of what is happening in our bodies and begin to relate physical feelings to our emotions. Practice kindness.	1, 2, 3, 4
6. Finding Your Feelings	See Hear Feel	Learn to relate physical feelings to our emotions. Practice kindness.	1, 2, 3, 4,
7. Finding Your Feelings Story	Finding Our Feelings Story	Practice relating physical feelings to our emotions. Practice kindness.	1, 2, 3, 4

Unit 3 – Empathy in Action			
Week	Mindfulness Skill	Lesson Objective(s)	CASEL Competencies*
8. Heartfulness	Heartfulness Practice	Use the practice of thinking kind thoughts to increase feelings of compassion and empathy for yourself and others. Practice kindness.	1, 2, 3
9. The THiNK Test	Head, Shoulders, Knees, and Toes	Learn about mindful speaking. Practice kindness.	1, 2, 3, 4, 5

10. Putting the THiNK Test to Work	See, Hear, Feel	Practice mindful speaking: thinking before you speak. Practice kindness.	1, 2, 3, 4, 5
11. Getting Bullied	SEL Story	Help us to see a story from different perspectives. Help to build the courage, skills and confidence to stand up for ourselves and others. Practice Kindness.	1, 2, 3, 4, 5
12. The Role of the Bystander	SEL Story	Help us to see a story from different perspectives. Help to build the courage and confidence to stand up for ourselves and others. Practice Kindness.	1, 2, 3, 4, 5
13. Understanding Bullying Behavior	Heartfulness	Help us to see a story from different perspectives. Help to build the courage and confidence to stand up for ourselves and others. Practice Kindness.	1, 2, 3, 4, 5

Unit 4 – Gratitude and the Negativity Bias			
Week	Mindfulness Skill	Lesson Objective(s)	CASEL Competencies*
14. Hacking your Brain	Web of Gratitude	Learn about the Negativity Bias and how we can "hack" our brains to reduce its power. Practice kindness.	1, 2, 3, 4, 5
15. Sergio's Scales	Web of Gratitude	Practice gratitude to balance the brain's negativity bias. Practice kindness.	1, 2, 3, 4, 5
16. Gratitude Cards	Web of Gratitude	Practice gratitude. Recognize how expressing gratitude makes you feel. Practice kindness.	2, 3, 4

Unit 5 – Brain Science			
Week	Mindfulness Skill	Lesson Objective(s)	CASEL Competencies*
17. Rosie's Brain	Student choice: Take Five, Four Square Breathing, Clench and Release or Gravity Hands	Re-introduce students to their brains via a story. Introduce a new mindfulness game. Practice kindness.	1, 2, 3, 4, 5
18. Brain Review	Student choice: Take Five, Four Square Breathing, Clench and Release or Gravity Hands	Deepen understanding of how three parts of our brain, the amygdala, the hippocampus, and the prefrontal cortex, operate in regulating our emotions and reactions to stimuli. Practice using real-life scenarios. Practice kindness.	1, 2, 3, 4, 5

| 19. Your Brain and Basketball | Student choice: Take Five, Four Square Breathing, Clench and Release or Gravity Hands | Review how three parts of our brain, the hippocampus, the amygdala and the prefrontal cortex, play a role in regulating our emotions and reactions to stimuli. Practice kindness. | 1, 2, 3, 4, 5 |

Unit 6 – Conflict Resolution

Week	Mindfulness Skill	Lesson Objective(s)	CASEL Competencies*
20. Conflict Escalator: Swings are for Babies	Student choice: Take Five, Four Square Breathing, Clench and Release or Gravity Hands	Review the concept of a **Conflict Escalator** (developed and named by William Kreidler). Help children understand how and why conflicts get worse. Practice kindness.	1, 2, 3, 4, 5
21. MOFL: Apology Practice	What do you Feel?	Understand what makes a good apology. Practice apologizing. Practice kindness.	1, 2, 3, 4, 5
22. Conflict Toolbox Matching Game	Student choice: Take Five, Gravity Hands, Clench and Release, Four Square, See, Hear, Feel	Practice with the Conflict CAT. Practice kindness.	1, 2, 3, 4, 5
23. Conflict CAT Role Play	Student choice: Take Five, Gravity Hands, Clench and Release, Four Square, See, Hear, Feel	Practice Conflict Resolution skills taught in previous lessons. Practice kindness.	1, 2, 3, 4, 5
24. Create Your own Conflict Resolution Scenarios	Student choice: Take Five, Gravity Hands, Clench and Release, Four Square, See, Hear, Feel	Integrate skills learned over the entire year to solve conflicts skillfully. Practice kindness.	1, 2, 3, 4, 5
25. Conflict CAT Game	Student choice: Take Five, Gravity Hands, Clench and Release, Four Square, See, Hear, Feel	Practice Conflict Resolution skills taught in previous lessons. Practice kindness.	1, 2, 3, 4, 5

Unit 7 – The Story I'm Telling Myself

Week	Mindfulness Skill	Lesson Objective(s)	CASEL Competencies*
26. Remote Control Mindfulness	Remote Control Breathing	Become aware of when minds wander. Practice noticing thoughts. Practice kindness.	1, 2, 3, 4, 5
27. Where Are My Thoughts	Past-Present-Future	Notice if thoughts are mostly about the past, present or future. Practice kindness.	1, 2, 3, 4, 5
28. Fast and Slow Thinking	Past-Present-Future	Learn about Fast and Slow Thinking and relate the concept to earlier lessons. Explore how Fast and Slow Thinking can be both	1, 2, 3, 4, 5

		helpful and challenging. Practice kindness.	
29. Don't Believe Everything You Think	Remote Control Breathing	Learn about and discuss implicit bias and stereotypes. Practice kindness.	1, 2, 3, 4, 5
30. Gender Stereotyping	Remote Control Breathing	Learn about and discuss gender stereotypes. Practice kindness.	1, 2, 3, 4, 5
31. Using Mindfulness to Interrupt Bias	Heartfulness	Help to build the courage, confidence and skills to stand up for ourselves and others. Practice kindness.	1, 2, 3, 4, 5

Unit 8 – Closing out the Year			
Week	Mindfulness Skill	Lesson Objective(s)	CASEL Competencies*
32. The Kindest Things	Heartfulness	Encourage the children to see the good in each other and experience the good feeling of sharing heartfelt compliments.	3, 4
33. Capstone Project	Choose your own practice	Support students in summing up what they have learned this year. Have students consider how they will put their new skills to work.	1, 2, 3, 4, 5

*Correlation with the five Core SEL Competencies identified by the Collaborative for Social Emotional Learning (CASEL.org)

1. Self-Awareness
2. Self-Management
3. Social Awareness
4. Relationship Skills
5. Responsible Decision Making

IV. Preparing to Teach Fourth and Fifth Grade

Introducing this Curriculum

The key message we recommend sharing with 4th and 5th graders is: These practices are tools to help you manage your own emotions, understand and control your reactions, build stronger friendships, and solve conflicts skillfully. *This is for you.*

If you are teaching students who have had **the *Peace of Mind Core Curriculum for Grades 3-5*,** or are already familiar with mindfulness, here are a few suggestions to keep in mind as you introduce this curriculum to your students:

- Recognize your students' experience, and introduce this as a more advanced year of practice.
- Invite experienced students to help new students.
- Point out what's the same: Mindfulness Helper, Kindness Pals, some mindfulness practices, some lesson topics.
- Point out what's new: topics such as the embodiment of feelings, addressing bullying and bias; new mindfulness practices and games; all new skits, all new stories; the possibility for deeper discussions thanks to their own growth and development.
- Remind students that this practice is their own. The more they invest, the more powerful it can be for them.

Expectations

We are not looking for perfection or final mastery from our students, but rather engagement and growth in the practice of mindfulness and kindness to others and ourselves.

Keep your expectations reasonable. Sometimes the kid who is sitting with his eyes wide open, legs jiggling, and fiddling with a pencil—but not talking—during mindfulness practice is doing his very best and is benefiting greatly from the effort. The exercises in this curriculum are for the benefit of the children and, as long as it is not preventing other children from practicing, a little moving around is ok.

Engagement

There may be students in your classroom who are reluctant to engage fully in mindfulness practice because they think it isn't cool or have some sort of negative attitude toward mindfulness. If this is the case, it can be very helpful to relate mindfulness to sports. Many sports teams and sports stars such as the Seattle Seahawks, Kobe Bryant, and Lebron James practice mindfulness regularly to enhance their performance. Talking about how mindfulness practice can help us play better by helping us focus, control our temper, be more of a team player, connect our minds and bodies, and calm our nerves can be very influential to student athletes.

This can also be true of music, dance, and just about anything else that your students are interested in. Finding the relevance can be important, especially for the older elementary students.

You might remind your students that they always have a choice about whether to practice mindfulness or not. It is a personal practice. If they choose not to, that is fine, as long as they do not prevent their peers from practicing. Encourage them to stay with the group and just sit quietly and think about whatever they want to think about while the others are doing the mindfulness practice. Often knowing that they have the freedom to opt out will allow kids to opt in.

You might like to focus on the power these practices give us to take care of big emotions, to focus our attention, to decide how to respond to a given situation. These are skills for life that allow your students to learn to control themselves, so others don't need to step in to control them.

When children practice these tools, they also have what they need to build stronger, more positive relationships with friends and family. They can be peace teachers in the way that they act and respond to situations and people around them.

Finally, it may help to consider that you are planting and nurturing seeds that will mature at different times – perhaps long after the school year is over.

Trauma Sensitive Teaching

One important area of growth in our field is in the area of trauma-sensitive mindfulness teaching. While mindfulness can be tremendously helpful for most people, for some, certain practices may trigger traumatic responses. These responses might range from discomfort and twitchiness to intense memories of a traumatic event. As teachers, our role is to notice our children's responses, to remind them that they always have a choice about whether to do a certain practice or not, to offer an alternative, to be flexible, and to seek help when we feel out of our depth.

Here are a few guidelines that we hope will be helpful to you in your teaching:

- Remember, offering choice is essential, and can be especially helpful in engaging older elementary students.
- Be flexible with points of focus, invite open or closed eyes, allow some flexibility with body position and movement, as long as adaptations for one child do not compromise the ability of other children to practice.
- Reassure children they can stop a practice anytime, or choose another practice as long as it doesn't interfere with anyone else's practice.
- Notice what is happening for your students as they practice. Check in with children who seem uncomfortable, and offer a quiet alternative.
- Seek additional help if needed.

We encourage you to learn more about this area. Here are two excellent resources: *Trauma-Sensitive Mindfulness: Practices for Safe and Transformative Healing* by David Treleaven and *The Trauma Sensitive Classroom* by Patricia Jennings.

Modeling what you teach

Students will take their cues from you. It is so important to establish your own mindfulness practice before you attempt to teach it to your students, and to continue to be open to learning along with your students. You don't have to be an expert in mindfulness but it is important to join your students on the journey.

You may have already found resources that support you in teaching the **Peace of Mind Curriculum**. If not, there are a few good ones listed in the Resource area of the Appendix and in the Educator section of the **Peace of Mind** website. TeachPeaceofMind.org

Unit 1
Welcome to Peace Class

Week 1
Welcome to Peace Class!

OBJECTIVES: Review the concept of mindfulness and re-establish the foundation for mindfulness practice

Launch Kindness Pals for the year

PREPARE: A bell or chime

Your Kindness Pals list and Talking Object

Worksheet: Who is my Kindness Pal?

Welcome to Peace Class! In this first Unit, we focus on introducing (or re-introducing) some foundational mindfulness practices, and invest time in building community through our Kindness Pals practice. In fact, all lessons in the curriculum begin with mindfulness practice led by a mindfulness helper and close with Kindness Pals. This structure will feel familiar to students who have had *Peace of Mind* before.

We suggest that you give all children a chance to be the Mindfulness Helper, moving through your class list. Some kids will need more prompting than others; see script below. There is a sheet in the **Materials for Lessons** section to help you keep track of your Kindness Pal pairings each week. The goal is for all children to be paired with everyone in the class by the end of the year. You can make pairings strategically, or simply go down your student list, changing pals every week.

Peace of Mind is not intended to control students' behavior, but instead to teach students the skills to self-regulate and to make skillful decisions about how they speak and act so that they are able to realize their goals.

As this is their own practice, you might begin by reminding your students that they always have a choice about whether to participate in a given mindfulness practice. Offering choice is an important trauma-sensitive practice, respecting a child's ability to choose what feels safe to them. We hope they will try, but if a student prefers not to try the practice, you might offer them an alternative that doesn't interfere with their classmates' practices, such as walking quietly back and forth across the back of the room if they need to move or sitting quietly and thinking about something else (but not reading or doing another activity).

We hope that over the course of the year students are able to hone their skills in paying mindful attention, building compassionate relationships, and solving conflicts peacefully. We are not looking for perfection or final mastery, but rather engagement and growth in the practice of mindfulness and kindness, to ourselves and others.

If you are wondering about the best ways to engage your students in this curriculum, you might like to review the suggestions under "Engagement" in the previous section.

If this curriculum is new to you, you may want to watch the video that demonstrates Take Five Breathing, the mindfulness practice you will teach in this lesson. You can watch it beforehand or watch it with your class and learn the practice together. It's up to you! https://TeachPeaceofMind.org/students-2/

Enjoy!

Introduction

You might say: *Welcome to Peace Class! We are going to be spending time [again] this year learning about mindfulness, kindness, and conflict resolution.*

Can anybody remind us what mindfulness means? **Take some answers.**

Sometimes we get confused about what that word actually means. Sometimes people think it means being quiet, or kind, or calm. But really it just means to be paying attention.

Let's say we are walking into a room. How can we walk into the room mindfully?

Do we have to walk in quietly? Well, sometimes we do. If we are walking into the library, then it would be mindful to walk in quietly because people are reading and the library is a quiet place.

How about when we walk into a birthday party? **Take some answers.**

Do we have to walk in quietly or can we walk in chatting with friends and saying "Hello!" to people? Noticing where we are and thinking about how we should be in that place is being mindful.

How about when we are eating? What does it mean to eat mindfully? **Take some answers.**

Do we have to eat quietly? Maybe, but mostly it just means to notice what we are eating. What does it taste like, smell like, look like, feel like? It would be polite to eat quietly but that isn't always the same thing as being mindful.

We learn to become more mindful by doing our mindfulness practice. That's when we are quiet because we are paying attention to what is happening in our own minds and bodies. Practicing paying attention to what is happening in our minds and bodies makes it easier for us to be mindful of the world around us. So let's get ready to start a (another) year of learning to be more mindful!

———

If your class is familiar with mindfulness, ask the class these questions, and take some answers. Otherwise skip to next "Say" prompt.

- Did anybody practice mindfulness over the summer?
- Did you use deep breathing to help you to calm down when you were angry or sad or nervous?

That's great! This year we will continue to practice those things because it takes a long time to start to remember to use your mindfulness skills.

———

Say: *Even people who have been practicing mindfulness for many, many years still do the same practices that we will do in Peace Class. They sit quietly and try to focus on their breath just like we do. That's because everyone's minds really want to wander and it takes a lot of continued practice to help our minds to focus on one thing at a time.*

Remember that we can practice mindfulness anywhere we go. We don't need any equipment, everything that we need is right here in our own bodies.

So, let's dive in!

Mindfulness Practice

Say: *Let's get into our Mindful Bodies. What does that mean to you?*

Take a few answers. *Yes, sitting up tall but comfortably, hands in lap, eyes closed or open looking down into your lap or at the floor in front of you.*

Say: *(Just like last year) We are going to have a Mindfulness Helper every week. The Mindfulness Helper will choose someone to turn the lights off and on, will say "Let's get into our mindful bodies; Let's close our eyes or look down; Let's take three deep breaths." The Mindfulness Helper will ring the bell at the end of our practice.*

Choose a Mindfulness Helper (MH).

Ask the MH to choose someone to turn off the lights. Encourage the class to be happy for the person who is chosen, perhaps waving hands in a silent show of appreciation. Point out that we have a choice about how to respond - why not be supportive? Everyone will all have a turn.

Prompt the MH to say: *"Let's get into our mindful bodies; Let's close our eyes or look down; Let's take three deep breaths."*

Introduce Take Five Breathing

Say: *Has anyone recently heard someone say "Take five?" Usually Take Five means to take a break - usually a five-minute break.*

Ask: *Do you remember how we "Took Five" last year?* **Take a few answers.**

Say: *Let's review it together. Hold up your hand like you are going to give someone a high five with your palm facing out and your fingers spread wide. Now take the index finger of your other hand and trace the outline of your hand.*

What does it feel like when your finger runs between your fingers? Maybe a little tickly?

We're going to do this again, but this time we are going to breathe in when we are tracing up and breathe out when we are tracing down.

Starting with your index finger down by your wrist, on the outside of your thumb, trace up your thumb slowly. As you trace up, breathe in and as you trace down the inside of your thumb, slowly breathe out.

Repeat this motion with all of your fingers until you are back down at your wrist on the outside of your pinky finger. At this point you will have taken five deep breaths.

Say: *Now let's take one more deep breath in and out. Let's listen to the sound mindfully and open your eyes or look up when you can't hear it anymore.*

Ask the MH to ring the bell.

Ask the MH to choose a classmate to turn the lights on.

Ask the MH to return to his or her seat.

Say: *Take Five is a great way to help you calm down, anytime you need a break.*

Kindness Pals

Introduce Kindness Pals as follows:

If necessary, say: *Since you've had Peace of Mind before, you will probably remember how this works.*

Otherwise start with: *Every time we meet, I am going to give you a Kindness Pal. It will be a different person in your class each time. I'm going to ask you to do something kind for this person between now and the next time we meet.*

Ask*: What are some examples of things you could do for Kindness Pals?* **Take some answers.**

Say*: So, your kind acts can be something small like stacking your pal's chair or something bigger like drawing them a picture, making them a card, or playing with them at recess. You can even do more than one thing.*

Ask*: Can you think of other kind things you could do for your Kindness Pal?* **Take some answers.**

Say*: I have one very important rule about Kindness Pals. (If appropriate, ask: Who remembers this rule?)* **Take some answers.**

Since the whole point of Kindness Pals is to help us practice being kind, I want to make sure that we start out with kindness. So when I tell you who your Kindness Pal is going to be, I want you to say "okay" to me in a friendly way. Let's try that all together: "Okay!"

When I tell you who your Kindness Pal is, you might feel really happy and excited. Maybe your Kindness Pal is already your really good friend, and it will be really easy to be kind to them.

But sometimes when I tell you who your Kindness Pal is, you might feel differently. You might feel a little nervous or shy. And that's fine. Any way that you feel is fine. But in that moment I want you to try really hard to be kind to your Pal and say a friendly "Okay!" to me. That way your Pal will know that you are ready to show them some kindness.

Ask*: Do you have to be friends with your Pal?* **Call on a hand or two.**

That's right. You don't have to become friends with your Pal (although you might), and you don't even have to like your Pal. All I'm asking you to do is to find some way to be kind to them this week.

When we meet next time, I'm going to ask you to try to remember something that you did for your Kindness Pal and share it with the class. Are you ready to find out who your Kindness Pal is?

Read through the list, saying, for example, "Rosie and Henry are Kindness Pals."

Wait for the "Okay" before moving on.

Say: *Now that you know who your Kindness Pal is, you are going to find out a little more about them. Who has a question that we could ask our Kindness Pal?*

Listen to students' suggestions. They might suggest asking about their favorite color or favorite food or sport.

Invite the Class to do a Kindness Pal Challenge

Say: *I'm going to set a timer for 90 seconds. You're going to sit with your Kindness Pal and try to find out how many things you two have in common. Remember to ask each other questions and keep track. When I ring the bell we'll share what we found out about each other.*

You can let the time go longer than 90 seconds if the kids seem to be having a good time.

Share. Come back together as a group and ask them to share something that they learned about their Kindness Pals. This exercise is a great way to practice Mindful Listening and help them to develop an interest in others.

Hand out copies of the *Who is my Kindness Pal* worksheet.

Say: *Now that you have gotten to know your Kindness Pal a little bit, you are going to do this worksheet. You will:*

- draw a picture of your kindness pal;
- write down some things that you have learned about them;
- make a plan for some of the kind things you could do for them this week.

Give them time to finish.

Say: *Okay, so now we've gotten to know our Kindness Pal a little better. I can't wait until next time when we get to hear about the kind things you did for your Pal. Have fun!*

Closing words: *Thanks for a great class, everyone. Let's have a nice quiet moment with the bell. You can close your eyes or leave them open but let's sit quietly and listen to the bell. If you want to, you can THiNK about your new Kindness Pal and imagine yourself doing something kind for them.*

Ring the bell or chime.

Extensions

Writing Prompts:

Can you think of a time when Take Five Breathing might be helpful to you? Write about it.

What did you learn about your Kindness Pal that surprised you?

What are some kind things you could do for your Kindness Pal this week?

At Home:

Practice Take Five Breathing and notice when it might be helpful to you.

Teach a family member or friend Take Five breathing and explain to them how it might help them.

Week 2
My Kindness Pal's Favorite Things

OBJECTIVES: Learn a new way of practicing mindfulness

Practice kindness

PREPARE: A bell or chime

A Talking Object

Your Kindness Pals list

Worksheet: My Kindness Pal's Favorite Things

This week your students will spend some time getting to know their new Kindness Pal a little better. In this lesson you are going to assign the Kindness Pals just after Mindfulness Practice and they are going to interview each other using the My Kindness Pal's Favorite Things Worksheet. Establishing the Kindness Pals as a consistent part of each week helps your students begin to know and connect with each other, contributing to a more positive and cooperative class climate.

Introduction

Say: *Today you are going to get a chance to get to know your new Kindness Pal a little bit better. You are going to be interviewing each other to find out about each other's favorite things.*

First, let's do our Mindfulness Practice.

Mindfulness Practice

Choose a Mindfulness Helper (MH).

Ask the MH to choose someone to turn off the lights. Encourage the class to be happy for the person who is chosen.

Prompt the MH to say: *"Let's get into our mindful bodies; Let's close our eyes or look down; Let's take three deep breaths."*

Say: *Let's do Take Five Breathing.*

Starting with your index finger down by your wrist, on the outside of your thumb, trace up your thumb slowly. As you trace up, breathe in and as you trace down the inside of your thumb, slowly breathe out.

Repeat this motion with all of your fingers until you are back down at your wrist on the outside of your pinky finger. At this point you will have taken five deep breaths.

After a few moments, say: *Now let's take one more deep breath in and out. Let's listen to the sound mindfully and open your eyes or look up when you can't hear it anymore.*

Ask the MH to ring the bell.

Ask the MH to choose a classmate to turn the lights on.

Ask the MH to return to his or her seat.

Kindness Pals

Say: *Would anyone like to share something kind you did for your pal last week?*

Pass the talking object to a few students who wish to share and have them pass it to their Kindness Pal who can either share what they did or say "thank you" to their Pal.

Assign new Kindness Pals.

Pass out one copy of the Worksheet to each pair and ask them to sit together facing each other.

Go over the questions on the worksheet and make sure everyone understands the questions.

Say: *When I say go, you are going to start to interview each other. You can take turns asking each other questions (What is your Favorite movie?) and then go on to the next question.*

Sometimes people get stuck on thinking of a favorite thing. If you don't have a favorite book or movie or food just name one that you really like.

Also try to share the "Whys." Why do you like spaghetti? Why is Peace of Mind Class your favorite part of the school day? ;) Try to listen really carefully to your partner's answers.

When we are finished with the interviews I'm going to ask you to share some of what you learned about your Kindness Pal.

Okay, let's get started.

This might take 15-20 minutes although some kids will be done quickly. If kids are done too quickly, you might ask them to think of some bonus questions, offer some additional questions yourself, or ask them to go more into the "whys."

Share: Go through each question on the sheet and ask for some students to share what they learned about their Kindness Pal.

Ask: Was anybody surprised about what they learned about their Pal? Did you find out that you had things in common that were unexpected?

Closing words: *Thanks for a great class, everyone. Let's have a nice quiet moment with the bell. You can close your eyes or leave them open, but let's sit quietly and listen to the bell. If you want to, you can think about your new Kindness Pal and imagine yourself doing something kind for them.*

Ring the bell or chime.

Extensions

Writing Prompts:

How did you use Take Five Breathing in the last week?

What are some of your favorite things that you didn't get to share?

What other questions would you wished you had asked your Pal about their Favorite Things?

What are some of the kind things you could do for your Kindness Pal this week?

At Home:

Interview a family member or friend about their Favorite Things.

Are their answers what you expected?

Week 3
What Works for You?

OBJECTIVES: Notice how your body responds to different practices and what is most helpful to you

Practice kindness

PREPARE: A bell or chime

A talking object

Your Kindness Pals list

Means to show a video to your class

Copies of the Same and Different worksheet found in the **Materials for Lessons** Section

Mindfulness practice is a very personal thing. What works for one person may not work for another. *Peace of Mind* aims to help students develop their own practices that meet their own individual needs. In this lesson we introduce three practices that, in addition to Take Five breathing, can be used to help calm down when you are angry. They are: Gravity Hands, Clench and Release, and Four Square Breathing. Today and later in the curriculum, students will be given the opportunity to choose their own practices during the Mindfulness portion of the lesson based on what they feel will serve them best in the moment.

There are videos on our website that demonstrate Four Square Breathing and Gravity Hands (https://TeachPeaceofMind.org/students-2/) among others. Mindful hip-hop artist JusTme has a video that demonstrates Clench and Release. http://www.yomind.com/justme (#7)

You can show these videos to your class or you can watch them yourself and then teach the practice. It's up to you!

Introduction

Say: *Today we are going to learn a few new ways to practice mindfulness. These are all things you could do to help to calm yourself down when you get angry or upset.*

There are so many different ways of doing this. I encourage you to experiment with them and even come up with your own. It can make your mindfulness practice more fun to mix it up and try new things.

I'm going to introduce the practices first, and then we'll ask our Mindfulness Helper to set us up so we can try them.

1. **Gravity Hands**

   Say: *Gravity Hands is a really simple practice to help you to focus while you take three deep breaths.*

   Show the video https://TeachPeaceofMind.org/students-2/) if you think this would be helpful.

   Or Say: *To do gravity hands, you start with your hands on your knees with your palms facing up. As you slowly breathe in, lift your hands up just about to shoulder height and then slowly turn them over and lower them as you breathe slowly out. We call this Gravity Hands because you are lifting your hands so slowly that you might feel the gravity of the earth pulling them back down. As you are lowering your hands, you want to resist gravity and bring them slowly down. This slow hand movement can help you to THiNK about breathing very slowly.*

   Let's try it! **Try it a couple of times.**

   Okay, we'll get back to Gravity Hands, but now I want to show you another way of doing calming breathing.

2. **Four Square Breathing:**

   You might say: *When I was a kid we used to play a game called Four Square at recess. Do any of you play it? This is a little different.*

   Show the video if you choose: (https://TeachPeaceofMind.org/students-2/)

   Say: *Four Square breathing is another fun way to take deep breaths to help you to calm down. To do Four Square breathing, draw an invisible square in the air in front of you. Imagine that you are starting in the bottom left hand corner of your square. As you breathe in you draw a line up while you slowly count to four. Then you hold your breath as you draw a line across the top and slowly count to four. Then you breathe out as you draw a line down and slowly count to four. Then you wait as you draw a line across the bottom connecting the lines of the square and slowly count to four.*

Let's try it! **Try it a couple of times.**

Now we're going to learn one more.

3. **Clench and Release:**

    You might say: *Here is one more you might like.*

    Show the video *if you choose: http://www.yomind.com/justme (Practice #7)*

    Say: *Clench and Release is a great way to help you to calm down because it not only helps you to take slow deep breaths but it also allows you to relax your body which sometimes becomes tense and tight when you get angry or upset.*

    Starting with your hands you will breathe in and squeeze your hands tightly (not so tight that it hurts) and count to 3 and then slowly breathe out for 3 counts as you slowly relax your hands. Then move around to different parts of your body - shoulders, feet, face, stomach, and so on.

    Let's try that for a moment.

Mindfulness Practice

Say: *When the Mindfulness Helper says: "Let's take three deep breaths" you can choose which one of these new practices you want to try out.*

Invite today's Mindfulness Helper (MH) to come to the front of the class to sit next to you on a chair.

Prompt the MH to choose another student to turn off the classroom lights.

Prompt the MH to say: "Let's get into our mindful bodies. Close your eyes or look down into your lap. Let's take 3 deep breaths."

Say: *Okay now you can choose which one you want to try out - Gravity Hands, Four Square, or Clench and Release.*

Wait about 15 seconds or a bit longer if it looks like they are comfortable.

After a few moments, say: *Now let's take one more deep breath in and out. Let's listen to the sound mindfully and open your eyes or look up when you can't hear it anymore.*

Ask the MH to ring the bell.

Ask the MH to choose a classmate to turn the lights on.

Ask the MH to return to his or her seat.

Ask some children to share which practice they chose and why? How did it feel?

Turn and Talk

Invite the students to: *Turn to someone next to you and share the practice you chose. Tell your partner why and how it felt. As always, make sure that everyone around you has a partner. We don't want anyone to be left out.*

Kindness Pals

Sharing Acts of Kindness

Say: *Would anyone like to share something kind you did for your pal last week?*

Pass the object to a few students who wish to share and have them pass it to their Kindness Pal who can either share what they did or say "thank you" to their Pal.

Take a few moments to let the children share what they did for their Kindness Pal during the past week.

Activity: Same and Different

Say: *Today we're going to do another activity that will help you to get to know your new Kindness Pal. You're going to spend a little time getting to know each other and then you are going to write and draw about it.*

Assign New Kindness Pals.

Hand out a Worksheet to each student.

Say: *When I say go, you and your Kindness Pal are going to get together with your Worksheets and a pencil. You are going to try to find at least three ways that you are the same on the outside and at least three ways that you are different on the outside.*

Then you are going to try to find at least three ways that you are the same on the inside and at least three ways that you are different on the inside.

How are we going to find ways that we are the same and different on the outside?

- With our eyes.

How are we going to find ways that we are the same and different on the inside?

- By talking to each other and listening to each other.

Give them 10-15 minutes to work on the activity together and then bring them back together and have a few children share what they found.

Closing

Okay our time is up for today. Thank you for a great class, everyone. Let's have a nice quiet moment for the bell. If you want to, you can close your eyes, picture your new Kindness Pal, and imagine yourself doing something kind for them this week.

Ring the bell.

Extensions

Writing Prompts:

Which practice did you find most helpful? How did it make you feel?

How are you and your Kindness Pal the same on the inside and different on the outside?

What are some of the kind things you could do for your Kindness Pal this week?

At Home:

Teach a family member or friend one of the mindfulness practices you learned today.

Try using one of the practices you have learned at home or at one of your activities.

Week 4
See, Hear, Feel

OBJECTIVES: Learn a new way of practicing mindfulness

Practice kindness

PREPARE: A bell or chime

A Talking Object

Your Kindness Pals list

Copies of the See, Hear, Feel Worksheet found in the **Materials in Lessons** Section

Today we introduce a new mindfulness practice called "See, Hear, Feel." This practice engages all of the kids' senses by asking them to notice first what they see (with eyes open or closed); then what they hear in the environment; and then what they feel in their body (sensations). Remember you can use any of the mindfulness practices we have learned so far at other times during the school week when you need to help kids - or yourself! - calm big emotions or focus attention.

Introduction

Say: *Today we are going to try a new mindfulness practice called See, Hear, Feel.*

See, Hear, Feel is another way of doing mindfulness. In this practice we are just going to be paying attention to three things - what we see, what we hear, and what we feel in our bodies. We'll be sitting quietly with our eyes closed or looking down at the floor or our laps. When I say "See," you're just going to try to notice what you are seeing.

Let's try it now: Just close your eyes or look down at the floor or your lap. What are you seeing right now? If your eyes are closed you might see lights or shapes or you might see images of things you were looking at or thinking about. **Wait about five seconds**. *What did you see?*

Take some answers.

Next I will say "Hear" and you can notice all of the sounds that you hear.

Let's try that now: Let's close our eyes again or look down and try to keep your body really still so that you aren't making any noises. **Wait about five seconds**. *What did you hear?*

Take some answers.

Next I will say: "Feel". This time we are going to be trying to notice feelings or sensations in your body. Sensations are feelings you have in or on your body. You might have an itch that you want to scratch or your hand might feel tingly. Your stomach might feel hungry or you might feel like you need to go to the bathroom. Those are all sensations in your body. Those are different but often related to emotions. Right now we are trying to focus on the sensations or body feelings.

Let's try that now: Let's close our eyes again or look down and try to keep your body really still. **Wait about five seconds.** *What did you feel?*

Take some answers.

So that's how you do See, Hear, Feel. So let's try it out! But first, let's invite our first Mindfulness Helper to help us get set up.

Mindfulness Practice

Invite today's Mindfulness Helper (MH) to come to the front of the class to sit next to you on a chair.

Prompt the MH to choose another student to turn off the classroom lights.

Prompt the MH to say: "Let's get into our mindful bodies. Close your eyes or look down into your lap. Let's take 3 deep breaths."

Say: *Let your breath settle back into its natural rhythm. You don't have to change it at all.*

So remember, all I am going to say is See, Hear or Feel. You're going to try to move your attention around to focus on those things that you see, hear and feel.

Don't worry if you get distracted and start thinking about something else. That's totally normal. As soon as you notice that your mind went somewhere else just try to start again. This might happen a bunch of times and that's fine.

See… wait about ten seconds

Hear… wait about ten seconds

Feel…. wait about ten seconds

Repeat this two or three times - if the students seem restless cut it shorter.

Okay, great job! Let's take one big deep breath and reach your arms up over your head as you breathe in and slowly float them down as you breathe out.

After a few moments, say: *Now let's take one more deep breath in and out. Let's listen to the sound mindfully and open your eyes or look up when you can't hear it anymore.*

Ring the bell to end the session or just ask them to open their eyes and/or look up.

Ask the MH to choose a classmate to turn the lights on.

Ask the MH to return to his or her seat.

Reflect and Discuss

1. **Write or Draw**

    Hand out the worksheet to each student. Invite them to write or draw what they saw, heard and felt.

2. **Turn and Talk**

    Assign new Kindness Pals so they can do this activity together.

    Share with Kindness Pal what they each saw, heard and felt.

    Direct them to take turns: first one person shares what they saw, and then the other.

    Repeat with "Hear" and "Feel."

3. **See, Hear, Feel Chart**

    Draw a chart on the board with three columns.

    Label the tops of each columns "See" "Hear" and "Feel."

    Ask the class:
    - Who would like to share what they were seeing?
    - Who would like to share what they were hearing?
    - Who would like to share what they were feeling?

    Take a few answers for each question and write answers on the chart you have hung or drawn on the board.

    Notice what students had in common, and the range of different answers. **Emphasize** that there are no right answers here; everyone's practice is uniquely their own.

Kindness Pals

Say: *Would anyone like to share something kind you did for your pal last week?*

Pass the object to a few students who wish to share and have them pass it to their Kindness Pal who can either share what they did or say "thank you" to their Pal.

Invite the Class to do a Kindness Pal Challenge

Say: *I'm going to set a timer for 90 seconds. You're going to sit with your Kindness Pal and try to find out how many things you two have in common. Remember to ask each other questions and keep track. When I ring the bell, we'll share what we found out about each other.*

You can let the time go longer than 90 seconds if the kids seem to be having a good time.

Share. Come back together as a group and ask them to share something that they learned about their Kindness Pals. This exercise is a great way to practice Mindful Listening and help them to develop an interest in others.

Say: *Okay, so now we've gotten to know our Kindness Pal a little better. I can't wait until next time when we get to hear about the kind things you did for your Pal. Have fun!*

Closing words: *Thanks for a great class, everyone. Let's have a nice quiet moment with the bell. You can close your eyes or leave them open but let's sit quietly and listen to the bell. If you want to, you can think about your new Kindness Pal and imagine yourself doing something kind for them.*

Ring the bell or chime.

Extensions

Writing Prompts:

How did you feel before we did See, Hear, Feel? How did you feel after?

What Favorite things did you and your Kindness Pal have in common?

What are some of the kind things you could do for your Kindness Pal this week?

At Home:

Teach a family member or friend the See, Hear, Feel practice.

Unit 2
Learning our Body's Language

Week 5
Flashlight Body Scan

OBJECTIVES: Learn that we can be aware of what is happening in our bodies and begin to relate physical feelings to our emotions

Practice kindness

PREPARE: A bell or chime

Your Kindness Pals list and Talking Object

This lesson introduces a method of body scanning that you can use over and over again. It helps the children tune into what is happening in their bodies and their feelings.

This is a good time to remind your students that they always have a choice about whether to participate in a given mindfulness practice. We hope they will try, but it is always up to them. If you notice a child who is looking uncomfortable, remind them quietly that they have a choice about whether to participate. Offer them some alternatives that will not disturb others, such as choosing another practice, walking quietly at the back of the room if they really need to move, or just sitting quietly and thinking about something else until the practice is done. Try not to give them the option of doing something else like reading. Most kids will get something out of the practice just by sitting and being part of the group experience. Sitting quietly for a few minutes doing nothing can be a very healthy break for some kids.

As with any lesson in this curriculum, you can use this script to begin, and then adapt it to make it your own in the future.

Introduction

If applicable, ask: *Does anyone remember the body scan we learned to do last year?*

Notice the show of hands.

Say: *This year we are going to learn a type of body scanning called "Flashlight Body Scanning." In a few minutes we are going to ask our Mindfulness Helper to get us set up for Mindfulness practice. After we take our three deep breaths, I will guide you through the Flashlight Body Scan.*

Mindfulness Practice

Invite today's Mindfulness Helper (MH) to come to the front of the class to sit next to you on a chair.

Prompt the MH to choose another student to turn off the classroom lights.

Prompt the MH to say: "Let's get into our mindful bodies. Close your eyes or look down into your lap. Let's take 3 deep breaths."

Say: *Today we are going to take a little trip around our bodies with our minds.*

Take your time with this and talk softly. Remind your students that it's okay if they don't feel anything; the important thing is just to try.

Remind them that you will be asking them questions but that they will be answering the questions in their own minds silently and that we will share later.

Use this script:

Today we are going to do a Flashlight Body Scan. You can lie down if you feel comfortable doing that; otherwise you may sit in a chair.

Close your eyes and try to make your body so still that the only thing you can feel moving is your breath. Imagine that you have a big flashlight hanging over your body. Imagine that you can operate this flashlight with your mind. Turn it on. Turn it off. Turn it on again.

Move it so that it is shining on your feet. Move it so that it is shining on your head. We're going to use the flashlight to help us to focus on different parts of our bodies.

Start by shining the flashlight on your right foot. Notice if you can feel any sensations there. Is it warm…. cold…. itchy…. do you feel your sock? Does it feel soft or scratchy? Are your shoes tight or loose?

Now move your flashlight to your left foot. Do you notice any differences? Is it warmer or colder than your right foot? What do you notice?

Now move your flashlight up to your knees. What do you feel there? Can you feel the fabric of your pants or leggings? Can you feel the air on your knees?

Now move your flashlight to your right hand. Can you still feel the tingling feeling from the big clap or has that gone away? Does your hand feel cold or warm, dry or a little sweaty?

Now move your flashlight to your left hand. What is different over there? Is one hand warmer than the other? How does your left hand feel?

Now move your flashlight to your belly. There is always something going on in your belly so it's a good place to notice sensations. Maybe it's almost time for lunch and you can feel that your stomach is empty. Maybe you have just eaten lunch and you can feel your food digesting. Maybe you can feel your belly rising and falling with your breath. Try to notice that for a few breaths.

Now move your flashlight to your chest. Maybe you can feel your heart beating. Maybe you can feel your chest rising and falling as your lungs fill up with air and empty again. Try to notice that for a few breaths.

Now move your flashlight up to your face. Shine it on your right eye. What do you feel there? What does it feel like to have your eyelid closed? Move it to your other eye? Any differences?

Move your flashlight to your nose. Can you feel the air going in and out? Maybe you can't. Just try to notice it.

Move your flashlight to your mouth. Focus on your tongue. What does it feel like? Is it dry or wet? Is it itchy?

Move your flashlight to your teeth. Can you feel your teeth without touching them with your tongue? If you have braces you definitely know what your teeth feel like when your braces have been tightened. How do you know that you have teeth if you can't see them?

Move your flashlight to the top of your head. Can you feel your hair with your mind?

Now pull your flashlight back so that it is shining on your whole body. What do you notice? Maybe you are feeling really relaxed and could lie here all day. Maybe you are feeling antsy and can't wait to get up. Any way that you feel is fine. Just try to notice what it feels like.

After a few moments, say: *Now let's take one more deep breath in and out. Let's listen to the sound mindfully and open your eyes or look up when you can't hear it anymore.*

Ask the MH to ring the bell.

Ask the MH to choose a classmate to turn the lights on.

Ask the MH to return to his or her seat.

Reflect and Discuss

Ask the students to open their eyes. Use these questions to guide a discussion.

- What did it feel like to travel through your body?
- What did you notice?
- Are you used to paying attention to your body?
- Would it be helpful to pay more attention to your body?
- What about when you are playing a sport?
- What about when you are in school?

Kindness Pals

You can include some or all of the following as time allows, but do assign new Kindness Pals.

- Share kind acts from the previous week.
- Assign new Kindness Pals.
- Do the Kindness Pal Challenge (see Week 4)
- Share what you learned about your Kindness Pal with the group.

Closing words: *Okay our time is up for today. Thank you for a great class, everyone. Let's have a nice quiet moment for the bell. If you want to, you can close your eyes, picture your new Kindness Pal, and imagine yourself doing something kind for them this week.*

Ring the bell.

Extensions

Writing Prompts:

What was the Flashlight Body Scan like for you? How did it make you feel? What surprised you?

What are some of the kind things you could do for your Kindness Pal this week?

At Home:

If you liked the Flashlight Body Scan, try it at home.

Week 6
Finding Your Feelings

OBJECTIVES: **Learn to relate physical feelings to our emotions**

                             Practice kindness

PREPARE: **A bell or chime**

                             Your Kindness Pals list and Talking Object

                             Your Kindness Pal list

                             Copies of the Find Your Feelings worksheet for each student from the Materials for Lessons Section

Our bodies have a way of capturing and reflecting our emotions that is different for each of us. The more we learn to pay attention to physical sensations in our bodies and their relationship to what we are feeling, the greater our ability to notice and reflect on our feelings before acting on them.

When kids are acting out and discussing emotions in this lesson, it might be helpful to point out:

- *Excitement* is a clenched, upward emotion. We tend to gasp when we are excited.
- *Anger* is a clenched and downward emotion. Our bellies feel tight and uncomfortable; we sometimes make fists.
- *Excitement and anger* feel similar in some ways. You might ask students to point out how they feel similar and how they feel different.
- *Sadness* is a downward emotion. Our bodies are not clenched but it's not a relaxed feeling either. Point out expressions like "feeling down" or "down in the dumps". Sadness feels low energy whereas excited feels high energy.
- *Happy* is usually a relaxed, open, pleasant feeling. There's no tightness in the belly and we're likely to have relaxed breathing. Sometimes kids confuse happy with overjoyed or excited. Ask children to point out the differences in how these emotions feel in their bodies.
- *Nervous* is a down and clenched feeling. Point out expressions like "butterflies in your stomach."

Understanding the language of our bodies can be a powerful tool to help us navigate our responses to challenging situations and emotions.

Introduction

You might say:

Today we are going to explore where we feel emotions in our bodies. Sometimes we call emotions "feelings." That can be confusing as "feeling" also means sensation.

When we've been doing See, Hear, Feel, we've been focusing on feeling sensations, like itchiness.

Today are going to be talking about feeling emotions, like anger and happiness. When we feel an emotion, we also feel a sensation in our bodies that goes with it.

But first, our mindfulness practice.

Mindfulness Practice

Invite today's Mindfulness Helper (MH) to come to the front of the class to sit next to you on a chair.

Prompt the MH to choose another student to turn off the classroom lights.

Prompt the MH to say: "Let's get into our mindful bodies. Close your eyes or look down into your lap. Let's take 3 deep breaths."

Repeat "See, Hear, Feel" Practice from Week 4.

After a few moments, say: *Now let's take one more deep breath in and out. Let's listen to the sound mindfully and open your eyes or look up when you can't hear it anymore.*

Ask the MH to ring the bell.

Ask the MH to choose a classmate to turn the lights on.

Ask the MH to return to his or her seat.

Lesson: Finding Your Feelings

1. **Act it Out**

Say: *Now we're going to explore where we feel emotions in our bodies. For example, when I feel the emotion of anger, I feel a sensation here in my body.*

Point to where you are most aware of your own anger.

Explain that you are going to invite volunteers to come to the front of the class and you will whisper an emotion to them.

Emotions to act out: angry, sad, happy, scared, excited, nervous, grouchy, cheerful, relaxed, confident, confused, embarrassed, shy, silly, proud, discouraged, jubilant, enraged, panicky, miserable, terrified, ecstatic.

Invite students to act out the emotion you whisper to them by saying "Today is Tuesday" and using their body and their voice to convey the emotion. The other students will guess what emotion they are portraying.

> *NOTE: Some of these emotions are complex and might be new words for your students. Take some time to define the words and list them on the board. It's so important for children to learn vocabulary to help them to express their feelings.*

Help kids focus on what they see in each other's bodies that give them a clue.

Ask them to point out the similarities and differences between emotions such as excited, nervous and scared.

2. **Emotions and Sensations**

   Say: *Now we're going to be focusing on how some of these emotions feel in our bodies. You've seen people act out some emotions, but they might feel different in your own body. Let's make a list of some of the emotions we acted out and then make a list of body sensations we feel when we have those emotions.*

   Draw the following on the board. Have the kids brainstorm two lists - one of emotions and one of sensations.

   <u>***Emotions***</u>   <u>***Sensations***</u>

   Invite the students to see if they can make connections between the emotions and the related sensations.

   You might say: *What sensations do you feel in your body when you are angry?*

   Draw a line connecting the emotion on the left with all of the sensations that students suggest they feel.

Example:

Emotions	_Sensations_
Angry	upturned corners of mouth
Nervous	clenched fists
Scared	stomach ache
Excited	butterflies in the stomach
Happy	warm and tingly
Impatient	
Calm	

(Angry → stomach ache; Nervous → butterflies in the stomach; Scared → clenched fists)

You might say: *Not everyone will feel the same emotion in their bodies in exactly the same way. It's our job to learn our own body's language so that we can take care of our own needs and understand ourselves.*

Ask: *Where do you feel happiness?*

> **Take a few answers**, and highlight answers that are not the same. **You might say**, for example:
>
> "So John feels happiness in the way his face relaxes, but Yoab notices his arms and legs feel lighter when his is happy. What's important is that John and Yoab both know how their bodies feel when they are happy, not that they feel it in the same way."

Ask: *Where do you feel anger?*

> **Take a few answers**, and highlight answers that are not the same. **You might say**, for example:
>
> "So Marlene feels clenching in her stomach when she begins to get angry, but James feels his face heat up when he is angry. It's ok to notice different things in our bodies. What's important is that Marlene and James both know how their bodies feel when they are angry."

Ask: *Why is it important to notice where we feel emotions in our bodies?*

> **Take a few answers, and then say:**
>
> *One of the reasons to notice where we feel emotions in our bodies is that it can help us to take care of our emotions.*
>
> *When we don't notice a feeling like anger or sadness, it can get bigger and bigger and possibly cause us to take actions that don't make things better.*
>
> *Our bodies often give us the first clue to what emotion we are feeling. If we learn to pay attention to what we are noticing in our bodies, we can often understand more quickly what emotion we are having.*

If you can notice, for example, anger when it is just a small feeling in your belly or a small clench of the fists, then you can use your mindful breathing skills to take care of it.

Here's an important thing to understand: **we're not trying to get rid of our emotions; we're just trying to take care of them**. *If we can notice that we're angry or sad or nervous when those feelings are small, then we can take steps to do something about what is making us feel that way. Our bodies can help us notice.*

We'll continue to talk about where we feel our feelings next time.

Kindness Pals

Do the Kindness Pals activity. You can include some or all of the following as time allows, but do assign new Kindness Pals:

- Share kind acts from the previous week.
- Assign new Kindness Pals.
- Do the Kindness Pal Challenge (see Week 4).
- Share what you learned about your Kindness Pal with the group.

Closing words: *Okay our time is up for today. Thank you for a great class, everyone. Let's have a nice quiet moment for the bell. If you want to, you can close your eyes, picture your new Kindness Pal, and imagine yourself doing something kind for them this week.*

Ring the bell.

Extensions

Writing Prompts:

How could paying attention to where you feel emotions in your body help you?

What are some of the kind things you could do for your Kindness Pal this week?

At Home:

Practice noticing where you feel emotions in your body.

Ask a friend or family member where they feel it in their bodies when they are happy, sad, mad or excited. Do they know? Is it the same place that you feel these things, or different?

Week 7
Finding Your Feelings Story

OBJECTIVES: Learn to relate physical feelings to our emotions

Practice kindness

PREPARE: A bell or chime

Your Kindness Pals list and Talking Object

Today we are going to continue to learn about the connection between our emotions and sensations in our bodies. For mindfulness practice, you are going to read a story and ask the children to imagine that they are the main character. You will ask them to notice how they would feel - both emotion and body sensation - at different points in the story. Helping students tune into their bodies this way can be so helpful in developing an "early warning system" that helps kids manage emotions before they are overwhelmed.

Introduction

You might say:

Today we are going to continue exploring where we feel emotions in our bodies. I'm going to tell you a story that might contain some scenes that are familiar to you, and you'll be able to see where you feel emotions in your body as we go.

Mindfulness Practice

Invite today's Mindfulness Helper (MH) to come to the front of the class to sit next to you on a chair.

Prompt the MH to choose another student to turn off the classroom lights.

Prompt the MH to say: "Let's get into our mindful bodies. Close your eyes or look down into your lap. Let's take 3 deep breaths."

Finding Your Feelings Story

Say: *Today I am going to tell you a story. I want you to imagine that you are the main character in the story and imagine how you would feel.*

At different points in the story I am going to stop and ask you to point to where you feel emotions in your body. For instance, if you feel mad in the story, you might point to your eyebrows or your mouth or your belly.

Don't worry if you don't notice anything. Just give it a try. There are no right or wrong answers! Remember, I am going to be asking you questions but you are going to answer them silently in your mind. You will have a chance to share our answers when we are finished with the story.

Say:

Imagine that you are lying in bed and you wake up and realize that it is time to go to school. How do you feel? Point to where you feel it.

You're about to get up when you remember that it's Saturday. How do you feel? Point to where you feel it.

You decide to go back to sleep and you snuggle up and get comfy. How do you feel? Point to where you feel it.

Suddenly you remember that you are going to a birthday party today. How do you feel? Point to where you feel it.

You look out the window and notice that it is raining. The birthday party was supposed to be at a park. How do you feel? Where do you feel it?

You decide to get up and read for a little while. You're in the middle of a really good book and you want to get back to it. How do you feel? Where do you feel it?

But you can't find your book anywhere. How do you feel? Where do you feel it?

You remember that your sister said that she really wanted to read that book. How do you feel? Where do you feel it?

You decide to go into your sister's room and demand your book back. How do you feel? Where do you feel it?

When you get out of bed you trip over your book. How do you feel? Where do you feel it?

You get up and walk into the kitchen. Your family is eating breakfast. There are pancakes for breakfast. How do you feel? Where do you feel it?

You accidentally drop a pancake and your dog drags it away to eat in her dog bed. How do you feel? Where do you feel it?

Your mom says that she has to work and can't drive you to the party. How do you feel? Where do you feel it?

Your mom says that your friend's dad is going to pick you up and take you to the party. How do you feel? Where do you feel it?

It's time to go to the party but you can't find your lucky sweatshirt that you like to wear almost every day. How do you feel? Where do you feel it?

Your brother says that you can wear his team jersey if you want. How do you feel? Where do you feel it?

You get to the party and the sun suddenly comes out. How do you feel? Where do you feel it?

Your friend opens the presents and really likes the present you made for him. How do you feel? Where do you feel it?

After a few moments, say*: Now let's take one more deep breath in and out. Let's listen to the sound mindfully and open your eyes or look up when you can't hear it anymore. Then you can open your eyes and sit up and we'll share how we felt during the story.*

Ask the MH to ring the bell.

Ask the MH to choose a classmate to turn the lights on.

Ask the MH to return to his or her seat.

Reflect and Discuss

Go through the story again line by line and give the kids a chance to share how they felt and where they felt it at each point in the story.

Assign new Kindness Pals so that they can pair share with their new Pals.

Ask the students to share with their new kindness pals how they were feeling in the story and to notice if they were feeling the same way or different ways.

Share with the Class.

Ask*: Did you notice any new connections between feelings and sensations that we didn't notice last time?*

Make sure to ask for different reactions. It's interesting to see how kids can have completely different emotional responses to the same events. Be sure to remind them that any way that they felt is fine.

Kindness Pals

Do the Kindness Pals activity. You can include some or all of the following as time allows:

- Share kind acts from the previous week.
- Kindness Pal Challenge (from Week 4).
- Sharing what you learned about your Kindness Pal with the group.

Closing words: *Okay our time is up for today. Thank you for a great class, everyone. Let's have a nice quiet moment for the bell. If you want to, you can close your eyes, picture your new Kindness Pal, and imagine yourself doing something kind for them this week.*

Ring the bell.

Extensions

Writing Prompts:

What do you remember from the story? When did you feel a strong emotion? What was it and where did you feel it?

What are some of the kind things you could do for your Kindness Pal this week?

At Home:

Notice what you are feeling in your body and where you feel it when you feel big emotions this week.

Ask someone else in your family what they notice in their bodies when they feel happy, sad, mad, or excited. Is it the same or different from what you notice in your body?

Unit 3
Empathy in Action

Week 8
Heartfulness

OBJECTIVES: Use the practice of thinking kind thoughts to increase feelings of compassion and empathy for yourself and others

Practice kindness

PREPARE: A bell or chime

Talking Object

Your Kindness Pals list

Heartfulness helps children strengthen their sense of compassion and empathy. It can also help them to let go of angry feelings they have toward others. In this lesson, kids will also develop "secret" handshakes with their kindness pals - which they'll then share with the class.

Introduction

Say: Today we are going to practice Heartfulness. You may remember practicing this last year, or perhaps you've practiced at home, too.

Practicing Heartfulness just means that we are going to be thinking about a person and thinking kind thoughts in our minds about that person.

Our Heartfulness practice can help us to develop something called Empathy. Does anybody want to guess what that word means?

Explain: Empathy is the experience of understanding another person's thoughts and feelings from their point of view, rather than from your own. You try to imagine yourself in their place in order to understand what they are feeling or experiencing.

Sometimes thinking kind thoughts about another person can help us to connect with them.

If applicable say: Last year we did Heartfulness for ourselves and other people that we care about. Today we are going to add to that and see what it feels like to think kind thoughts for someone we are a little bit mad at.

Say: *Sometimes doing Heartfulness for someone whom you are angry or frustrated with can help you to try to see things from their point of view, to remind yourself that they are a person too with thoughts and feelings and experiences that might be different from your own.*

Doing Heartfulness for someone doesn't mean that you necessarily like them or forgive them for what they did to make you angry. Remember that they don't know that you are thinking kind thoughts about them unless you tell them. The Heartfulness is really for you.

Sometimes doing the Heartfulness practice can change the way you feel about the person you are mad at. Maybe your brother was really annoying this morning but thinking kind thoughts for him makes you remember all of the good stuff he does too.

Sometimes Heartfulness can help you see why someone might have done what they did and you might feel differently about them. Sometimes you might not feel like forgiving that person and Heartfulness might just make your own feelings of anger easier to carry around. Just try it today and see what happens for you.

Remember that any way that you feel is fine. You are allowed to have all of your feelings.

Let's try it.

Mindfulness And Heartfulness Practice

Invite today's Mindfulness Helper (MH) to come to the front of the class to sit next to you on a chair.

Prompt the MH to choose another student to turn off the classroom lights.

Prompt the MH to say: "Let's get into our mindful bodies. Let's close our eyes/or leave them open, looking at the floor in front of you.. Let's take 3 deep breaths."

Heartfulness for someone who makes you happy

I'd like you to think about someone who makes you happy. Someone you see every day, at home or at school, could be someone in your family, a friend, a teacher, even a pet. Just choose someone and try to picture them happy and smiling. Picture them doing something that makes them happy. Try to notice how you feel when you think about this person.

Now, if you'd like to, put your hand over your heart and repeat these words in your mind while you think about this person:

May you be happy. **Wait a moment.**

May you be healthy. **Wait a moment.**

May you be peaceful. **Wait a moment**.

Take a moment to notice how you feel. Any way that you feel is fine, even if you feel nothing. Just try to notice it.

Heartfulness for yourself

Say*: This might feel a little strange, but this time we are going to send kind thoughts to ourselves. Imagine yourself happy and smiling, doing something that you like to do. Now repeat these words in your mind.*

May I be happy. **Pause**.

May I be healthy. **Pause**.

May I be peaceful. **Pause**

Again, try to notice how you feel. Does it feel different to send kind thoughts to yourself? Any way that you feel is fine. Just try to notice it.

Heartfulness for someone who you are a little bit mad at

Say*: Now I'd like you to think about someone you are mad at, or someone who made you feel sad. See if you can choose someone that you are just a little bit mad at. Maybe your brother ate the last bowl of cereal or your sister lost your page in the book you were reading. Not somebody who makes you really angry.*

Once you have chosen someone try to picture them happy and smiling. Picture them doing something that makes them happy. Try to notice how you feel when you think about this person. Remember, they can't hear you. You are just trying to notice how it feels to think these thoughts or feel these feelings. This is for you.

Now, if you'd like to, put your hand over your heart and repeat these words in your mind while you think about this person:

May you be happy. **Wait a moment.**

May you be healthy. **Wait a moment.**

May you be peaceful. **Wait a moment**.

Take a moment to notice how you feel. Any way that you feel is fine, even if you feel nothing. Just try to notice it.

After a few moments, say: *Now let's take one more deep breath in and out. Let's listen to the sound mindfully and open your eyes or look up when you can't hear it anymore.*

Ask the MH to ring the bell when the mindful breathing is complete.

Ask the MH to choose a classmate to turn the lights on.

Ask the MH to return to his or her seat.

Reflect and Discuss

Ask: What does it feel like to send kind thoughts to yourself? **Take a few answers.**

Say: *Sending Heartfulness to ourselves is not selfish. It is as important to treat ourselves with kindness as it is to treat others with kindness.*

Ask: When could you use Heartfulness to help yourself? **Take a few answers.**

Suggest: You can send Heartfulness to yourself when you feel sad, or sick, or worried.

Ask: *What does it feel like to send kind thoughts to people you care about?* **Take a few answers.**

Ask: *When could you send Heartfulness to someone else?* **Take a few answers.**

Suggest: You might send Heartfulness to someone you care about who is unhappy, or worried, or sick.

Ask: *What does it feel like to send kind thoughts to someone who you are mad at, or who made you feel sad?* **Take a few answers.**

Ask: *When could you send Heartfulness to someone you are mad at?* **Take a few answers.**

Suggest: You might send Heartfulness to someone you are mad at in order to help you find a solution to your conflict, and to help yourself feel more peaceful.

Kindness Pals

Share kind acts from the previous week.

Assign New Kindness Pals

Develop A Secret Kindness Pal Handshake

Say: Today we are going to be getting to know our new Kindness Pal in a new way. You are going to spend a few minutes finding out what you two have in common like we often do with our Kindness pal. But then you are going to create a Secret Kindness Pal Handshake.

Your handshake has to include:

- words, including at least five things that you have in common and
- at least five movements.

You'll have about ten minutes to do this and then we will share our handshakes with the class.

Share Secret Handshakes with the group.

Closing words: *Okay our time is up for today. Thank you for a great class, everyone. Let's have a nice quiet moment for the bell. If you want to, you can close your eyes, picture your new Kindness Pal, and imagine yourself doing something kind for them this week.*

Ring the bell.

Extensions

Writing Prompts:

What was it like to send Heartfulness to someone you care about? Someone you were a little bit mad at?

What are some of the kind things you could do for your Kindness Pal this week?

At Home:

Practice Heartfulness. Notice how you feel before and after you do this?

Teach Heartfulness to a friend or family member. Practice together.

Week 9
The THiNK Test

OBJECTIVE: Learn how to think before you speak

Practice kindness

PREPARE: A bell or chime

Your Kindness Pals list and Talking Object

Tyaja Uses the THiNK Test by Linda Ryden

Board or flip chart with this quote written clearly for all to read:

"Before you speak, ask yourself if what you are about to say is true, is helpful, is necessary, is kind. If the answer is no, then maybe what you are about to say should be left unsaid."

- Bernard Meltzer

Today we're going to learn a new mindfulness game called Head, Shoulders, Knees and Toes. If you are not familiar with how to play Head Shoulders Knees and Toes, watch this quick video to learn the song and see the mindfulness game version. You can also play the video for your class to teach this exercise if you prefer: https://TeachPeaceofMind.org/students-2/ This activity helps kids focus their attention, listen mindfully, and experience mindfulness in an active, joyful way.

Then we'll be learning (or reviewing) a tool for mindful speaking called the THiNK Test. We'll be reading and discussing a new book, *Tyaja Uses the THiNK Test*. You may have seen other versions of the THiNK Test. In our version, T stands for True, H stands for Helpful, N stands for Necessary, K stands for Kind, and the "I" stands for me, as in I think before I speak.

Mindfulness Practice

Mindfulness Challenge: the Head, Shoulders, Knees and Toes Game

You might say: *Today we are going to try a Mindfulness Challenge called The Head Shoulders Knees and Toes game. You probably already know how to play this game, but today we're going to be doing it a little bit differently. We're*

going to be doing it as a mindfulness game. So we're going to be playing the game mostly in our minds. Sounds weird, but let's try it.

Choose today's Mindfulness Helper.

Invite the MH to come to the front of the class to sit next to you on a chair.

Prompt the MH to choose another student to turn off the classroom lights.

Prompt the MH to say: "Let's get into our mindful bodies. Close your eyes or look down into your lap. Let's take 3 deep breaths."

Say: *Now we are going to play the game. The game has six levels. We'll see how many we can get to today.*

> **Level 1**: *I'll sing the song and we'll all do the gestures together with our hands while we sit in our mindful bodies with our eyes closed or looking down.*
>
> **Do Level 1.**
>
> **Level 2:** *I'll sing the song and you'll do the gestures but I'll change the rhythm a bit. Head……….. shoulders, knees and …………… toes, knees aaaaaaaaaaaand……… toes, and so on.*
>
> **Do Level 2.**
>
> **Level 3:** *I'll sing the song and you'll do the gestures but I will be changing the order a bit. I might say knees, toes, head and eyes, nose and mouth, for example.*
>
> **Do Level 3.**
>
> **Level 4**: *I'll sing the song but this time you won't do the gestures with your hands. You're going to pretend you have imaginary hands that are doing the gestures. Try to see if you can feel those parts of your body that you are touching with your mind.*
>
> **Do Level 4.**
>
> **Level 5:** *You will use your hands to do the gestures but I am NOT going to sing the song. You'll be singing the song in your head.*
>
> **Do Level 5.**
>
> **Level 6:** *This time you'll do all the work in your mind. You'll sing the song inside your mind and use your imaginary hands to do the gestures. Go slowly and see what you notice.*
>
> **Do Level 6.**

Say: *Now let's take one more deep breath in and out. Let's listen to the sound mindfully and open your eyes or look up when you can't hear it anymore.*

Ask the MH to ring the bell.

Ask the MH to choose a classmate to turn the lights on.

Ask the MH to return to his or her seat.

Reflect and Discuss

- What did you find easy?
- What did you find hard?
- Why did we call this a mindfulness exercise?
- How could playing Head Shoulders Knees and Toes help you?

Lesson: Mindful Speaking

1. **The THINK Test**

    Say: *Today we are going to be thinking about how we talk to each other. Have you ever said something and then right away wished that you hadn't said it? That has probably happened to all of us. Today we're going to learn a little trick that can help us to think before we speak so we don't end up saying things that we later regret.*

    Have this quote written on the board:

    > *"Before you speak ask yourself if what you are going to say is true, is kind, is necessary, is helpful. If the answer is no, maybe what you are about to say should be left unsaid."*
    > – Bernard Meltzer

    Have a few students read the quote from the board, one at a time. See if they can do it from memory.

    Ask the students what the quote means to them.

    Introduce the THINK test.

    Suggest to the students: *This is a great quote, but it's too long and hard to remember. It's easier when it's broken down a little bit. What do you think are the most important words in the quote?*

Take some answers until they come to these four - true, helpful, necessary, kind.

Write THNK on the board across in big letters and then write the words TRUE, HELPFUL, NECESSARY, KIND going down from the top under the corresponding letter.

Ask them what THNK spells? They will notice that it is THiNK without the "I".

Say: are you curious about what the "I" stands for? Let's find out by reading *Tyaja Uses the THiNK Test*.

2. **Read** *Tyaja Uses the THiNK Test.*

Reflect and Discuss

- How did the THiNK Test help Tyaja?
- Why didn't she think she needed the THiNK Test?
- What's the difference between a need-to and a want-to?
- Are there times when you definitely don't need to use the THiNK Test?
- Are there times when you always need to use the THiNK Test?
- Can you think of a time when you wished you had used the THiNK Test?

Say: *We'll talk more about the THiNK Test next time.*

Kindness Pals

Do the Kindness Pals activity. You can include some or all of the following as time allows, but do assign new kindness pals:

- Share kind acts from the previous week.
- Assign new pals.
- Kindness Pal Challenge.
- Sharing what you learned about your Kindness Pal with the group.

Ring the bell.

Closing words: *Thanks for a great class, everyone. Let's have a nice quiet moment with the bell. You can close your eyes or leave them open but let's sit quietly and listen to the bell. If you want to, you can think about your new Kindness Pal and imagine yourself doing something kind for them.*

Ring the bell or chime.

Extensions

Writing Prompts:

What questions do you have about the THiNK Test?

What are some kind things you could do for your Kindness Pal this week?

At Home:

Notice when you might be able to use the THiNK Test with family members or friends this week.

Week 10
Putting the THiNK Test to Work

OBJECTIVE: Practice mindful speaking - thinking before you speak

Practice kindness

PREPARE: A bell or chime

Your Kindness Pals list and Talking Object

Board/flip chart with this quote written clearly for all to read:

"Before you speak, ask yourself if what you are about to say is true, is helpful, is necessary, is kind. If the answer is no, then maybe what you are about to say should be left unsaid."

- Bernard Meltzer

In this lesson we are going to put the THiNK Test to work. The THiNK Test helps students pause before they are about to say something and make the choice to speak mindfully. Students will act out the parts of the THiNK Test as in the *Tyaja* book, and you and the other students will ask them questions. This lesson is similar to the one in the *Peace of Mind Core Curriculum for Grades 3-5,* but here we have new scenarios and questions for the THiNK Test to consider.

Introduction

You might say: *Today we're going to be practicing using the THINK Test that we learned about last week. I'll be choosing people to be Mr. True, Ms. Helpful, Mr. Necessary and Ms. Kind just like in the book* Tyaja Uses the THiNK Test. *We'll be asking them questions and seeing if what we want to say passes the THiNK Test.*

Mindfulness Practice

Invite today's Mindfulness Helper (MH) to come to the front of the class to sit next to you on a chair.

Prompt the MH to choose another student to turn off the classroom lights.

Prompt the MH to say: "Let's get into our mindful bodies. Close your eyes or look down into your lap. Let's take 3 deep breaths."

Do the "See, Hear, Feel" Practice from Week 4.

Say: *Say: Now let's take one more deep breath in and out. Let's listen to the sound mindfully and open your eyes or look up when you can't hear it anymore.*

Ask the MH to ring the bell.

Ask the MH to choose a classmate to turn the lights on.

Ask the MH to return to his or her seat.

Lesson: Mindful Speaking

1. **Using the THINK Test**

    Say: *Today we are going to practice putting the THiNK test to work. Let's review – what does THiNK Test stands for?*

    Take a few answers to arrive at:

    T: true

    H: helpful

    N: necessary

    K: kind.

    We use "I" as in "I think before I speak."

    Write THINK on the board across in big letters and then write the words TRUE, HELPFUL, NECESSARY, KIND going down from the top under the corresponding letter

    Talk about ways and times to use the THINK Test.

    Say: *Suppose you want to tell everyone in your class that you are having a birthday party this weekend. First ask yourself: does it pass the THINK test?*

    Talk about how the answer might be different if everyone in your class is invited or only a few kids are invited.

Try it with these scenarios too:

- You want to tell someone in your class that the book they are reading is for babies.
- You want to tell someone that her jeans are out of style.

2. **Role Plays**

   Choose four kids to represent the different words: Mr. True, Ms. Helpful, Mr. Necessary and Ms. Kind.

   Ask the representatives to try to help answer these and similar questions.

> NOTE FROM LINDA: *In my class I usually pretend that I want to say these things and then ask the THiNK test. For example I might choose four kids to be the THiNK Test and then I will say "Let's pretend that I am a fourth grader and I am on a soccer team and I think that our goalie isn't very good. I'm going to go and tell her that I think she shouldn't play goalie. Here I go… well maybe I should stop and check in with the THiNK Test first…" Then I ask the THiNK Test members individually what they think. "Mr. True, isn't it true that our goalie is no good?" and let Mr. True respond. I then ask kids in the class to weigh in on whether or not they agree with Mr. True (in a kind and constructive way). Then I go on to Ms. Helpful. Once this pattern is established you can ask a student to be the one asking the questions and then encourage students to think of their own questions for the THiNK Test.*

Repeat with a new group of four students.

- You want to tell someone on your soccer team that they are not a good goalie.
- You want to tell everyone that you got the solo in the choir concert.
- You want to tell someone that you just overheard a girl telling her friend that she has a crush on Kyle.
- You want to tell someone that their favorite YouTuber is inappropriate.
- You want to tell someone that you "like" them.
- You want to tell your teacher that your friend is getting bullied, but your friend told you not to tell anyone.
- You want to tell someone that their zipper is unzipped.

- Someone is spreading a rumor that your friend's parents are getting divorced and you want to tell them to stop.

Ask for more examples or take their questions.

Keep in mind that people may have very different interpretations of and answers to these questions. There is no one right answer. The purpose of this activity is to give kids a way to grapple with some tricky ethical questions.

Reinforce that it is okay if we don't all agree on the answers.

Kindness Pals

Do the Kindness Pal activities as time allows, but do assign new Pals:

- Share kind acts from the previous week.
- Assign new Kindness Pals.
- Do the Kindness Pal Challenge (see Week 4).
- Share what you learned about your Kindness Pal with the group.

Closing words: *Okay our time is up for today. Thank you for a great class, everyone. Let's have a nice quiet moment for the bell. If you want to, you can close your eyes, picture your new Kindness Pal, and imagine yourself doing something kind for them this week.*

Ring the bell.

Extensions

Writing Prompts:

Write about a time when using the THiNK Test might have helped you, or when you could use it in the future.

What are some kind things you could do for your Kindness Pal this week?

At Home:

Practice using the THiNK Test.

Explain the THiNK Test to a family member or friend and talk about how it might be helpful.

A note about bullying

We are about to head into a series of lessons focused on the challenging topic of bullying. You may be familiar with this generally accepted definition:

- Bullying is an action that is repeated.
- Bullying is an action that is intended to hurt another.
- The person doing the bullying has power over the target of the bullying in some way.

Let's explore what this means for your students.

Bullying is an action that is repeated. You may notice one-time acts of unkindness in your classroom - this is not bullying. Bullying is a pattern of behavior.

If it is bullying, the person doing the bullying is intentionally trying to hurt the other person. Sometimes children with invisible disabilities like autism may not fully understand the impact of their words and may hurt other people's feelings unintentionally. This is not bullying.

The person doing the bullying will have some sort of power over the person being bullied. This power could be due to being older or bigger or stronger. It could be due to being more academically successful or "popular".

Let's look for a moment at the role of the bystander when bullying is occurring. There is no such thing as a neutral bystander. The power of the person doing the bullying is enhanced by bystanders who say nothing and do nothing to help the person being bullied.

People who witness or are aware of bullying and do nothing about it are helping to bully the child who is targeted. Their silence can be interpreted by the person doing the bullying as support and approval and can be interpreted by the targeted child as agreement with the person doing the bullying.

You might have noticed that we do not use the term "bully" to describe the person doing the bullying. We use bully as a verb, not a noun. People who bully others are people who are making a choice. They can make better choices with guidance from adults. Other children can help, too, when they learn how to express their disapproval in ways that are kind but strong and do not escalate the situation.

In the following three lessons we will be learning about how children who are the targets of bullying can respond with the help of adults and other children.

We will learn how bystanders can learn about the importance of speaking up and how to do it. We will learn about why some people bully others and how they can learn to make better more positive and healthy choices. We will learn about empathy and the importance of hearing others' stories and having all of the facts before making a decision about someone.

All of these lessons are built on a foundation of mindfulness practice, and in particular, our ability to notice how our bodies feel in different situations. Noticing these feelings can help us to take care of challenging emotions before they escalate - a tremendously helpful skill when dealing with bullying.

Week 11
Getting Bullied

OBJECTIVES: Help us to see a story from different perspectives

Help to build the courage, skills and confidence to stand up for ourselves and others

Practice kindness

PREPARE: A real bell or chime

Your Kindness Pal List

Weird by Erin Frankel

In this lesson we read a book called *Weird*. *Weird* is the first book in a powerful trilogy of books called *Weird, Dare,* and *Tough* by Erin Frankel. These are some of the best books we know of to address issues of bullying, exclusion and inclusion. In the first book, *Weird*, the main character Luisa is repeatedly teased and called "weird" by her classmate Sam even though she is simply being herself. Luisa initially reacts to the bullying by withdrawing, but with the support of her teachers, parents, classmates, and friends, Luisa is able to resist Sam's unkind comments.

In this lesson, we ask students to pay attention to how their bodies react to hearing about bullying and kindness. Noticing where we feel emotions in our bodies can help significantly in taking care of big emotions before they escalate.

Please pay particular attention to the way your students react during the mindfulness practice. As with every lesson, be sure to remind students that closing eyes is optional.

Introduction

Say: *Today we are going to read a story called* Weird. *This is a story from the perspective of a girl named Luisa who gets bullied at school. This book deals with some real issues some of you may have experienced, and I'm looking forward to hearing your thoughts and ideas.*

First, though, let's start with our mindfulness practice. In this practice, I am going to describe some things that might happen in school or on the playground. I am going to ask you where you feel your reactions in your body.

Mindfulness Practice

Consult your alphabetical roll list, and choose the next student to be the Mindfulness Helper for the day.

Invite the Mindfulness Helper (MH) to come to the front of the class to sit next to you on a chair.

Prompt the MH to choose another student to turn off the classroom lights.

Prompt the MH to say: "Let's get into our mindful bodies. You may choose to close your eyes or look down into your lap. Let's take 3 deep breaths."

Say: *I'm going to describe a few different situations and I'd like you to imagine that they are happening to you. Try to notice how you feel and where in your body you feel it.*

- Imagine that you are playing with a few kids at recess, and somebody runs up and says something mean to your friend. Everybody except your friend laughs at what he says, including you. How do you feel? Where do you feel it?

- Now imagine that you are playing with a few kids at recess, and somebody runs up and says something mean to your friend. The other kids laugh, but you don't. You walk over to your friend and say "Let's get out of here." How do you feel? Where do you feel it?

- Imagine that you are playing with a few kids at recess and somebody runs up and says something mean to you. Everybody laughs except for you. How do you feel? Where do you feel it?

- Now imagine that you are playing with a few kids at recess and somebody runs up and says something mean to you. Everybody laughs except for one person. She comes over to you and says, "Let's get out of here." How do you feel? Where do you feel it?

- Imagine you are outside at recess and you run up to some kids and you say something mean to one of them. Everybody laughs except for the person you were mean to. How do you feel? Where do you feel it?

- Imagine you are outside at recess and you run up to some kids and you say something mean to one of them. Nobody laughs. How do you feel? Where do you feel it?

After a few moments, say: *Now let's take one more deep breath in and out. Let's listen to the sound mindfully and open your eyes or look up when you can't hear it anymore.*

Cue the MH to ring the bell when the mindful breathing is complete.

Cue the MH to choose a classmate to turn the lights on.

Ask the MH to return to his or her seat.

Ring the Bell.

Lesson: What is it like to be the target of bullying? How can we respond?

1. **Replay each situation and ask for people to share how they felt in different situations.**

   Ask:

   - Why might you laugh when someone says something mean, even if you don't think it's funny or you feel sorry for the person getting teased?
   - How did it feel when you were the one saying something mean and everybody laughed?
   - What did it feel like when nobody laughed?
   - How did you feel when you said to your friend "Let's get out of here?"

   Point out how our approval or disapproval can "train" people to keep doing things or stop doing things.

   Talk about how powerful it can be to stand there and not laugh.

2. **Read <u>Weird</u>.**

   Consider having children read the dialogue bubbles to engage them in the story.

   > *NOTE: If you have a Sam in your class you might choose to call the Sam character "Pam" or something else.*

Reflect and Discuss

To shape a discussion, you might ask:

1. What did Luisa do when Sam called her weird?
2. Did changing things about herself work? Did Sam stop bothering her?
3. Did Luisa handle this problem on her own or did she talk to other people?

4. What kind of advice did she get?
5. What did Luisa finally decide to do about Sam?
6. Did pretending she didn't care what Sam was saying work?
7. Do you think it would be hard to do what Luisa did?
8. Would this work if Sam were physically hurting her? The answer is no.

Say: *Next time we will learn the story of Jayla and see this story through her eyes.*

Kindness Pals

Kindness Pal Activity: You can include some or all of the following as time allows, but definitely assign new Kindness Pals.

- Share kind acts from the previous week.
- Assign new Kindness Pals.
- Do the Kindness Pal Challenge (see Week 4)
- Share what you learned about your Kindness Pal with the group.

Closing words: *Okay our time is up for today. Thank you for a great class, everyone. Let's have a nice quiet moment for the bell. If you want to, you can close your eyes, picture your new Kindness Pal, and imagine yourself doing something kind for them this week.*

Ring the bell.

Extensions

Writing Prompts:

Have you ever been the target of bullying? What was that like for you?

What are some of the kind things you could do for your Kindness Pal this week?

At Home:

In other books you are reading or in movies or TV shows you watch, look for examples of bullying and how it is handled. You might notice that what works on TV doesn't always work in real life.

Week 12
The Role of the Bystander

OBJECTIVES: Help us to see a story from different perspectives

Help to build the courage and confidence to stand up for ourselves and others

Practice kindness

PREPARE: A real bell or chime

<u>Dare</u> by Erin Frankel

Your Kindness Pals list

Today we will read *Dare*, the second book in the *Weird Dare Tough* Series. This time the story is told through the eyes of Jayla. When Jayla first witnesses Luisa being bullied, she is too scared to stand up for her, but soon she finds the courage to do what's right. These books help children see bullying through the perspective of the person who is the target of bullying, the bystander, and (next week) the person doing the bullying, fostering empathy, understanding and the courage to take a stand.

Introduction

You might say: *Last week we read about Luisa who was being bullied by Sam.*

This week, we're going to hear about the situation from Jayla's perspective. But first, let's do our Mindfulness practice. Like last class, I will read you some scenarios. Try to notice what you feel in your bodies as I read them.

Mindfulness Practice

Consult your alphabetical roll list, and choose the next student to be the Mindfulness Helper for the day.

Invite the Mindfulness Helper (MH) to come to the front of the class to sit next to you on a chair.

Prompt the MH to choose another student to turn off the classroom lights.

Prompt the MH to say: "Let's get into our mindful bodies. Close your eyes or look down into your lap. Let's take 3 deep breaths."

Say: *Remember the book that we read last time called* <u>Weird?</u> *I'm going to describe a few different situations and I'd like you to imagine that they are happening to you. Try to notice how you feel and where in your body you feel it.*

- Imagine that you are Luisa and you are wearing your favorite new polka dot boots to school and Sam shouts "Weird!" at you. How do you feel? Where do you feel it?

- Imagine that you are speaking Spanish to your Dad and Sam shouts "Weird!" at you. How do you feel? Where do you feel it?

- Imagine that you are Luisa and you have tried to change how you act and how you dress and how you talk and Sam still shouts "Weird!" at you. How do you feel? Where do you feel it?

- Now imagine that you are Luisa and you decide to just be yourself and ignore Sam. You come into school wearing what you want to wear and saying what you want to say. How do you feel? Where do you feel it?

- Imagine your friends support you and Sam backs down. How do you feel? Where do you feel it?

- Imagine you are Jayla and you've been watching Sam bully Luisa. How do you feel? Where do you feel it?

- Imagine you are Jayla. You give Luisa her boots back. How do you feel? Where do you feel it?

After a few moments, say: *Now let's take one more deep breath in and out. Let's listen to the sound mindfully and open your eyes or look up when you can't hear it anymore.*

Cue the MH to ring the bell.

Cue the MH to choose a classmate to turn the lights on.

Ask the MH to return to his or her seat.

Ring the Bell.

Lesson: The Role of the Bystander

1. **Replay each situation** and ask for people to share how they felt in different situations.

    Talk about where you feel different emotions in your body and why it might be helpful to start to pay attention to that. Talk about how it feels to be brave and how it feels to have the support of others.

2. Make Predictions

Say: *Today we are going to learn the story of Jayla. You might have noticed Jayla in the background of a lot of pictures in* Weird. *You might remember her as the one who gave Luisa her books back.*

Say: *Before we read* Dare, *let's make some predictions.*

- What do you think we are going to find out about Jayla?
- Why do you think it took her so long to help Luisa?
- Why do you think she didn't stand up to Sam?

Take a moment to think (give them a few moments of quiet).

3. Turn and Talk

Say: *Share your predictions with someone next to you and listen to theirs.*

Share Predictions with the Group

Write *the questions on the board and record the students' predictions.*

You might write *"Our Dare Predictions" on a piece of chart paper and then when the kids share a prediction, you can write in on a sticky note and ask the student to come up and put it on the chart. You can do this part any way that works best for you.*

After hearing *many of their predictions* **say**: *Okay let's find out more about Jayla. Let's read* Dare.

4. Read Dare.

Consider having students read dialogue bubbles to engage them in the story.

Reflect and Discuss

To shape a discussion, you might ask these questions pointing out or asking the kids to point out whether their predictions turned out to be true or not:

1. How did Jayla feel when Sam started bullying Luisa?
2. Why did Jayla go along with the mean things that Sam wanted her to do?
3. Have you ever felt pressured to do something mean?
4. Why did Sam have so much power over Jayla?

5. Did Jayla confront Sam on her own?
6. How did Sam react when Jayla refused to do what she wanted her to do?
7. How did Jayla's kindness affect Luisa?
8. How did Jayla get the courage to stand up to Sam?
9. Would the way Jayla acted in the book work in real life?

Say: *Next time we will learn the story of Sam and see this story through her eyes.*

Kindness Pals

Kindness Pal Activity: You can include some or all of the following as time allows, but definitely assign new Kindness Pals.

- Share kind acts from the previous week.
- Assign new Kindness Pals.
- Do the Kindness Pal Challenge (see Week 4).
- Share what you learned about your Kindness Pal with the group.

Closing words: *Okay our time is up for today. Thank you for a great class, everyone. Let's have a nice quiet moment for the bell. If you want to, you can close your eyes, picture your new Kindness Pal, and imagine yourself doing something kind for them this week.*

Ring the bell.

Extensions

Writing Prompts:

Have you ever been a bystander? How did it feel?

What are some kind things you could do for your Kindness Pal this week?

At Home:

Look for examples of bystanders in books, TV or movies and see how they act. How do they act? Would that work in real life?

Week 13
Understanding Bullying Behavior

OBJECTIVES: Help us to see a story from different perspectives

Help to build the courage and confidence to stand up for ourselves and others

Practice kindness

PREPARE: A real bell or chime

<u>Tough</u> by Erin Frankel

Your Kindness Pals list

This week, we read the final book in Erin Frankel's series: *Tough*. This book tells the story from the point of view of Sam, the girl who is treating the others badly. Notice that we talk in terms of the "person doing the bullying" rather than "the bully."

This lesson focuses on empathy: what is it and why is it important? For more information about the benefits of empathy and Heartfulness practice, you might like to read the article in the bibliography by Emma Seppala, Science Director, Stanford Center For Compassion and Altruism Research and Education, Co-Director Wellness, Yale Center for Emotional Intelligence, and author of *The Happiness Track*.

Introduction

Say: *Today we are going to read the last book in the Weird! Series. We are going to learn about Sam, and why she is treating Luisa and Jayla badly.*

Before we read the book we are going to do our Heartfulness practice. Today we are going to do our Heartfulness practicing thinking about Luisa, Jayla, and Sam. But first, let's talk about the book for a minute.

Ask:

- After reading *Weird* and *Dare* how do you feel about Luisa?
- How do you feel about Jayla?
- How do you feel about Sam?

Say: *So far we don't know much about Sam except that she acts in an unkind way toward other kids. So it would be understandable to feel angry with her or not to like her.*

Remember when we thought kind thoughts about someone that we were mad at? Thinking kind thoughts about Sam might be a little bit like that.

Our Heartfulness practice can help us to develop something called Empathy. Does anybody remember what that word means?

Review, if needed: *Empathy is the experience of understanding another person's thoughts and feelings from their point of view, rather than from your own. You try to imagine yourself in their place in order to understand what they are feeling or experiencing.*

Sometimes thinking kind thoughts about another person can help us to connect with them.

Sometimes Heartfulness can help you see why someone might have done what they did and you might feel differently about them. Sometimes you might not feel like forgiving that person and Heartfulness might just make your own feelings of anger easier to carry around. Just try it today and see what happens for you.

Remember that any way that you feel is fine. You are allowed to have all of your feelings.

Mindfulness Practice

Consult your alphabetical roll list, and choose the next student to be the Mindfulness Helper for the day.

Invite the Mindfulness Helper (MH) to come to the front of the class to sit next to you on a chair.

Prompt the MH to choose another student to turn off the classroom lights.

Prompt the MH to say: "Let's get into our mindful bodies. Close your eyes or look down into your lap. Let's take 3 deep breaths."

Say: *Today we are going to do our Heartfulness practice again. This is when we think kind thoughts about people in our mind. Today let's do our Heartfulness practice for Luisa, Jayla and Sam. This will help us to think about how they might feel and help us to feel empathy for them.*

Say: *Take a deep breath.*

First, Let's think about Luisa.

If you'd like to, put your hand over your heart and repeat these words in your mind while you think about this person:

May you be happy. **Wait a moment.**

May you be healthy. **Wait a moment.**

May you be peaceful. **Wait a moment**.

Take a moment to notice how you feel. Any way that you feel is fine, even if you feel nothing. Just try to notice it.

Next, Let's think about Jayla.

If you'd like to, put your hand over your heart and repeat these words in your mind while you think about this person:

May you be happy. **Wait a moment.**

May you be healthy. **Wait a moment.**

May you be peaceful. **Wait a moment**.

Take a moment to notice how you feel. Any way that you feel is fine, even if you feel nothing. Just try to notice it.

Finally, let's think about Sam.

If you'd like to, put your hand over your heart and repeat these words in your mind while you think about this person:

May you be happy. **Wait a moment.**

May you be healthy. **Wait a moment.**

May you be peaceful. **Wait a moment**.

Take a moment to notice how you feel. Any way that you feel is fine, even if you feel nothing. Just try to notice it.

After a few moments, say: Now let's take one more deep breath in and out. Let's listen to the sound mindfully and open your eyes or look up when you can't hear it anymore.

Cue the MH to ring the bell.

Cue the MH to choose a classmate to turn the lights on**.**

Ask the MH to return to his or her seat.

Ring the Bell.

Ask: *Does anybody want to share what you were feeling or thinking about?*

Take a few responses.

Lesson: *Tough*

1. **Make Predictions**

   Say: *Before we read* Tough, *let's make some predictions just like we did for* Dare.

   - What do you think we are going to find out about Sam?
   - Why do you think she is being so mean to Luisa and Jayla?

   Take a moment to think (give them a few moments of quiet).

2. **Turn and Talk**

   Say: *Share your predictions with someone next to you and listen to theirs.*

3. **Share Predictions with the Group**

   Write *the questions on the board and record the students' predictions.*

   You might write *"Our Tough Predictions" on a piece of chart paper and then when the kids share a prediction, you can write in on a sticky note and ask the student to come up and put it on the chart. You can do this part any way that works best for you.*

   After hearing *many of their predictions* **say**: *Okay let's find out more about Sam. Let's read* Tough.

4. **Read** Tough.

   Students might read the dialogue bubbles to engage them in the story.

Reflect and Discuss

To shape a discussion, you might ask these questions pointing out or asking the kids to point out whether their predictions turned out to be true or not:

- What did we learn about Sam's life at home that might explain why she is being unkind?
- Do you think Sam realized that she was being mean to Jayla and Luisa?
- How did Sam take care of her angry feelings?

- If Sam was learning about mindfulness, how could that have helped her deal with her angry feelings

Kindness Pals

Kindness Pal Activity: You can include some or all of the following as time allows, but definitely assign new Kindness Pals:

- Share kind acts from the previous week.
- Assign new Kindness Pals.
- Do the Kindness Pal Challenge (see Week 4).
- Share what you learned about your Kindness Pal with the group.

Closing words: *Okay our time is up for today. Thank you for a great class, everyone. Let's have a nice quiet moment for the bell. If you want to, you can close your eyes, picture your new Kindness Pal, and imagine yourself doing something kind for them this week.*

Ring the bell.

Extensions

Writing Prompts:

Did anything surprise you in the story *Tough*?

Does the story make you think differently about people whom you have seen being unkind to others?

What are some of the kind things you could do for your Kindness Pal this week?

At Home:

Try practicing Heartfulness at home.

Try practicing Heartfulness for someone you are mad at. Notice how it makes you feel.

Unit 4
Gratitude and the Negativity Bias

Week 14
Hacking Your Brain: Gratitude and the Negativity Bias

OBJECTIVES: Learn about the Negativity Bias and how we can "hack" our brains to reduce its power

Practice kindness

PREPARE: A bell or chime

Your Kindness Pals list and Talking Object

Sergio Sees the Good **by Linda Ryden**

The Negativity Bias refers to our brain's tendency to focus on and remember painful, embarrassing, or threatening experiences more than positive ones. The negativity bias can be helpful by protecting us from danger. For example, once we've experienced the sting of a bee, we are careful to avoid bees in the future. But have you ever focused so much on a minor negative experience - being late for an appointment, for example - that you've been unable to enjoy the good things going on around you for the rest of the day? If you have (and who hasn't?), you know all about the Negativity Bias.

Our book today, *Sergio Sees the Good,* shows us that unless we're in immediate danger, it's possible and more helpful to focus on the positive things in our lives.

Introduction

Say: *Today we're going to talk about the Negativity Bias. We're also going to read a new book called* <u>Sergio Sees the Good.</u>

But first, today we are going to try a new mindfulness practice that focuses on gratitude. Gratitude is the practice of noticing what we are thankful for, and expressing our thanks.

We are going to be creating a web of gratitude. We'll be thinking about people or things that we are grateful for and we'll be imagining that we are putting them in our web of gratitude. You can imagine little hearts that are like picture frames and put pictures of those for whom we are grateful in the heart frames.

Mindfulness Practice

Invite today's Mindfulness Helper (MH) to come to the front of the class to sit next to you on a chair.

Prompt the MH to choose another student to turn off the classroom lights.

Prompt the MH to say: *"Let's get into our mindful bodies; Let's close our eyes or look down; Let's take three deep breaths."*

Say: *So let's begin:*

Let's start by thinking about someone at home that you are thankful, or grateful for.

Think of someone who helps you and is kind to you. Imagine that they are in one of the little hearts in your web of gratitude.

As you breathe in, think "Thank you." As you breathe out, think "Thank you."

Next, let's Think about another kid at school. You might choose a friend or classmate who is kind to you. Imagine that they are in one of the little hearts in your web of gratitude. Let's send some thanks to that person.

As you breathe in, think "Thank you." As you breathe out, think "Thank you."

Now let's think about a grown up at school. Someone who is kind to you and helps you; someone you are grateful to have in your life. Imagine that they are in one of the little hearts in your web of gratitude. Let's send some thanks to that person.

As you breathe in, think "Thank you." As you breathe out, think "Thank you."

Maybe there is a special animal in your life such as a pet or a stuffed animal or an animal in the wild. Imagine that special animal in your web of gratitude.

As you breathe in, think "Thank you." As you breathe out, think "Thank you."

Now let's think about something in nature that you are grateful for. Maybe there is a special tree that you love or a flower or the ocean or the moon or snow, or something else. Choose something from nature to put into your web of gratitude.

As you breathe in, think "Thank you." As you breathe out, think "Thank you."

Now this time you can think about anyone or anything that you are feeling grateful to have in your life. Imagine adding that person or thing to your web of gratitude.

As you breathe in, think "Thank you." And as you breathe out, think "Thank you".

Take a moment to soak in this feeling of gratitude. Notice what it feels like in your body to be grateful and to say thank you. Remember that you can do this practice on your own anytime.

Let's take a deep breath in and stretch your arms up over your head and then slowly float your arms down as you breathe out. Let's listen for the sound of the bell and we'll open our eyes when we can't hear it anymore.

Say: *In a moment you will hear the sound of the bells and that will mean that it is time to open your eyes. So just get ready for that.*

Ask the MH to ring the bell.

Ask the MH to choose a classmate to turn the lights on.

Ask the MH to return to his or her seat.

Lesson: The Negativity Bias and *Sergio Sees the Good*

Ask: *Who knows what the role of the amygdala is?*

Take a few answers.

Say: *Yes, the role of the amygdala is to keep us safe. If we touch a cactus and get hurt, our brain will file that memory in order to prevent us from doing it again. That's helpful. Scientists call this the Negativity Bias. This means that our brains tend to focus on and remember negative things more than positive things.*

Say: *Most of the time, it would help us to focus more on the positive events in our lives. Of course, we remember the big good things like our birthday, or a great trip, or a special event. But we often forget all about small good things.*

Let's see what happened to Sergio.

Read *Sergio Sees the Good*

Reflect and Discuss

Ask: *How did the negativity bias affect Sergio?*

Take some answers. *Yes, he was miserable at the end of the school day.*

Ask: *What was Sergio's "brain hack?" How did he override the negativity bias?*

Take some answers. *Yes, he focused on the small good things, and noticed that they outweighed the bad things.*

Say: *The good news is, we can actually hack our brains to override our brain's negativity bias.*

Scientists have found that a great way to balance out our brain's tendency to focus on negative things is to take a moment to soak in positive things. Taking time to notice and really focus on something good that happens allows our brains to send those memories to long-term storage, and helps to train our brain to focus on the positive more often.

Focusing on the positive doesn't mean that we are trying to avoid negative things. Not at all. Our brains will take care of that for us. By helping our brains recognize and soak in positive things, we are helping our brains to see our lives more realistically.

Say: *We'll be thinking more about Sergio and the negativity bias next time.*

Kindness Pals

Kindness Pal Activity: You can include some or all of the following as time allows, but definitely assign new Kindness Pals.

- Share kind acts from the previous week.
- Assign new Kindness Pals.
- Do the Kindness Pal Challenge (see Week 4).
- Share what you learned about your Kindness Pal with the group.

Closing words: *Okay our time is up for today. Thank you for a great class, everyone. Let's have a nice quiet moment for the bell. If you want to, you can close your eyes, picture your new Kindness Pal, and imagine yourself doing something kind for them this week.*

Ring the bell.

Extensions

Writing Prompts:

Write a letter to one of the people in your web of gratitude to express your thanks.

What are some of the kind things you could do for your Kindness Pal this week?

At Home:

Notice when your brain's Negativity Bias may be preventing you from focusing on good things that happen.

Explain the Negativity Bias to a family member.

The real Ms. Snowden

Week 15
Sergio's Scales

OBJECTIVES: Practice gratitude to balance the brain's negativity bias

Practice kindness

PREPARE: A bell or chime

Enough small cups for every child in your class

You will need approximately 10 small identical objects for each child (such as marbles or pieces of macaroni). Divide objects into cups so that each **pair** of students may have one cupful.

Your Kindness Pals list and talking object

Building on last week's lesson about the brain's Negativity Bias, today's lesson gives children a chance to practice noticing the good things in our days in the way that Sergio did in last week's story. This practice can become a habit that can make us much happier and healthier in the long run. It's so important not to let our Negativity Bias be in charge all of the time and to really stop and notice all of the little good things that make up our lives.

Important: students may not choose to share every event in their day so far, and that is fine. As in all of our lessons, please respect children's decisions about how much to participate and share. If students seem overwhelmed by this, or do not think they have good things to share, help them notice the good things that might apply: warm socks or a sweatshirt on a cool day, being in class with a friend, a welcoming classroom, a caring teacher.

Today we also include a fun way to help your class focus on the positive: a call-and-response practice called "Tell Me Something Good." We invite you to sing it out! You will call on a student, and the whole class will sing "Tell me something good," inspired by the refrain popularized by recording artist Chaka Khan. The student will say one good thing that has happened recently. Then either you or the student will call on the next student by singing "Tell me something good." You may repeat until all students have had a turn.

Important! We are NOT recommending that you play the song for your class; it is not an appropriate song for elementary school. But you might want to check youtube for the tune if you would like to before class. Otherwise make up your own tune!

Introduction

Say: Today we are going to practice noticing and overriding our brain's negativity bias the way that Sergio did. But first, let's do our Web of Gratitude practice again.

Mindfulness Practice

Invite today's Mindfulness Helper (MH) to come to the front of the class to sit next to you on a chair.

Prompt the MH to choose another student to turn off the classroom lights.

Prompt the MH to say: *"Let's get into our mindful bodies; Let's close our eyes or look down; Let's take three deep breaths."*

Repeat the Web of Gratitude practice from Week 14.

After a few moments, say: *Now let's take one more deep breath in and out. Let's listen to the sound mindfully and open your eyes or look up when you can't hear it anymore.*

Ask the MH to ring the bell.

Ask the MH to choose a classmate to turn the lights on.

Lesson: Gratitude Practice

Say: *Does anyone remember how Sergio decided whether he was having a good day or a bad day?*

Take some answers.

Say: *That's right, he used marbles to represent moments in his day, and he put them either in the "good" or "bad" side of the scales.*

Ask: *What did Sergio find out after he filled the scales?*

Take some answers: *Yes. What he thought was a bad day was actually pretty good overall.*

Assign Kindness Pals so that they can work together on the next practice.

Say: *Now we are going to have a chance to practice this for ourselves with our Kindness pals. Please find a place to sit with your kindness pal.*

Ask a volunteer to hand out two empty cups and one cup full of objects to each pair. Have the children label their empty cups "good" and "bad."

Instruct: *Decide who will go first. The person who goes first will remember out loud everything about their day from the time they woke up. As the first person talks, their pal will put objects in either the "good" or "bad" cup for each event. When you have reached the present moment, take a minute to notice: has the day been more good or bad so far? When the first person has finished, return the objects to their starting cup. Then it is the other person's turn.*

Reflect and Discuss

Ask:

- Raise your hand if you found out they were having a bad day. A good day.
- Who was surprised by what you found?
- What were some of the good things you noticed?
- How did it feel to have your pal listening to you and putting marbles in cups for you?

Activity: Tell Me Something Good

Here's a fun activity to reinforce the habit of focusing on the positive. This is something you can use with your class anytime.

You might say: *Here's a fun way we can help each other remember the small good things. I'm going to call out one student's name, and then we are all going to sing to that student: "Tell Me Something Good." That student will say one good thing that has happened today. Then I'll choose another student, and we will all sing to that student. We will keep going until we have sung to everyone!*

Say: Emma! (a student's name)

All Sing: Tell Me Something Good.

Student says: I'm wearing my favorite socks! (or another good thing)

Teacher (or student) calls out next student's name. Repeat until all students have had a chance.

Kindness Pals

Kindness Pal Activity: You can include some or all of the following as time allows.

- Share kind acts from the previous week.
- Do the Kindness Pal Challenge (see Week 4).
- Share what you learned about your Kindness Pal with the group.

Closing words: *Okay our time is up for today. Thank you for a great class, everyone. Let's have a nice quiet moment for the bell. If you want to, you can close your eyes, picture your new Kindness Pal, and imagine yourself doing something kind for them this week.*

Ring the bell.

Extensions

Writing Prompts:

What is something that you are grateful for? Write about it.

What are some kind things you could do for your Kindness Pal this week?

At Home:

Practice Web of Gratitude
Notice how you feel before and after.

NOTE FROM LINDA: *Establishing a gratitude practice can be so important in helping to overcome the negativity bias and be happier. There are so many ways to do this.*

- *You can have gratitude journals that your students write in every day or once a week.*

- *You could have a Gratitude Box and ask your students to write something they are grateful for on a slip of paper and put it in the box and you could read out some of the slips once a week.*

- *You could have a gratitude challenge.*

Last year I did a Gratitude Challenge called Brush Up on Gratitude. I asked the kids to think of and write down three things they were grateful for every morning or night when they brushed their teeth. After 6 weeks I gave a small prize to the student who had the most things listed and another to the student with the most variety.

Week 16
Gratitude Cards

OBJECTIVES: Practice gratitude

Recognize how expressing gratitude makes you feel

Practice kindness

PREPARE: A bell or chime

Your Kindness Pals list and talking object

Index cards with the names and photos of all staff in your school

Materials with which to make gratitude cards

In this lesson, students will have a chance to express their gratitude to staff members in your school who support them every day. This exercise helps children realize how many people it takes to make a school run and helps to build the foundation for positive interactions in your school community.

Introduction

You might say: *Last week we sent our thanks and love to people in our lives to whom we felt grateful. Some of you sent gratitude to your parents, grandparents and friends.*

Today we are going to be saying thank you again, but this time to some important people in our lives right in our school building. I know that many of you have made birthday cards for your parents or maybe a thank you card for a favorite teacher.

But have you ever said thank you to our custodians? Or the front-office staff? Or the dedicated people who make our lunches in the cafeteria? Well, here's your chance!

Today we are going to show our thanks to these special people who keep our school running. I am going to give you an index card with somebody's name on it, and I'd like you to make that person a thank you card to express our gratitude for all of their hard work.

You might tell the kids that they can make a card for anyone they want as long as they first make one for the person on their index card.

Remind them how important it is for everyone to get a card—like on Valentine's Day when we make cards for everyone, not just the kids we like the best. If it's possible, have the children hand-deliver the cards.

Say: *As always, we'll begin with mindfulness practice to help us get ready.*

Mindfulness

Invite today's Mindfulness Helper (MH) to come to the front of the class to sit next to you on a chair.

Prompt the MH to choose another student to turn off the classroom lights.

Prompt the MH to say: "Let's get into our mindful bodies. Close your eyes or look down into your lap. Let's take 3 deep breaths."

Repeat Web of Gratitude Practice from Week 14.

After a few moments, say: *Now let's take one more deep breath in and out. Let's listen to the sound mindfully and open your eyes or look up when you can't hear it anymore.*

Ask the MH to ring the bell.

Ask the MH to choose a classmate to turn the lights on.

Ask the MH to return to his or her seat.

Say: *Take a moment to notice how you feel. Any way that you feel is fine, even if you feel nothing. Just try to notice it.*

> **NOTE:** *You may add on any other gratitude focus that you THiNK might be helpful to your class.*

Ask: What was that like for you?

Take a few answers.

Lesson: Gratitude Cards

Ask a volunteer to help distribute supplies: paper and crayons and markers.

Give out index cards with names of staff, custodians, and so on. If possible, include pictures of each person.

Invite students to make a card expressing gratitude for the person on their card.

Collect the cards when students are finished.

> *NOTE: Some kids may be really insistent about who they want to make a card for. Classroom teachers receive lots of thanks and kids always want to make a card for their favorite teacher from last year. Try to encourage them to spread that love, even to someone they don't know.*

Remind them that as with our Kindness Pals we can show kindness to people that we don't know very well. It's also important to remind them that everyone at the school is making an important contribution even though you might not be able to see it.

Kindness Pals

Kindness Pal Activity: You can include some or all of the following as time allows, but definitely assign new Kindness Pals.

- Share kind acts from the previous week.
- Assign new Kindness Pals.
- Do the Kindness Pal Challenge (see Week 4).
- Share what you learned about your Kindness Pal with the group.

Closing words: *Okay our time is up for today. Thank you for a great class, everyone. Let's have a nice quiet moment for the bell. If you want to, you can close your eyes, picture your new Kindness Pal, and imagine yourself doing something kind for them this week.*

Ring the bell.

Extensions

Writing Prompts:

Is there someone else at school you would like to write a gratitude card to? What would you say?

What are some of the kind things you could do for your Kindness Pal this week?

At Home:

Write a gratitude card to a member of your family, or another adult who is important to you, such as a coach.

Unit 5
Brain Science

Week 17
Rosie's Brain

OBJECTIVES: (Re-)Introduce students to their brains via a story
Introduce a new mindfulness game
Practice kindness

PREPARE: A bell or chime
Your Kindness Pals list and Talking Object
Rosie's Brain by Linda Ryden

Our brains are complex and quite amazing parts of our bodies. In this curriculum, we offer a simplified look at how our brains work in order to help children understand why we practice mindfulness and how it helps. We focus on two important components of the limbic system, the amygdala and the hippocampus, and also on the integrating portions of the brain's cortex, the prefrontal cortex.

We help 4th and 5th graders understand that there is more to the brain than these three parts, and explain that these three parts are interconnected with each other and the rest of the brain, even as we offer a helpful, basic overview of how these parts work together.

Today we'll be reading a book called *Rosie's Brain*. In this book, students will be introduced to three characters representing the amygdala, hippocampus and prefrontal cortex. Your students may remember acting out the *Rosie's Brain* skit in prior years if they had the *Peace of Mind Core Curriculum for Grades 3-5* before this year.

Today, our mindfulness practice will be an opportunity for the children to choose what they want to do. They will choose from the four "calming down" practices we have learned so far this year: Gravity Hands, Take Five, Four Square, and Clench and Release. This will help kids to remember ways to calm down when they get angry and help prepare them for working on resolving conflicts peacefully.

Introduction

Say: *Today we are going to read the book* Rosie's Brain *and learn a new game called Stop Walk Wiggle Sit. It's more challenging than it might sound! But let's start with our Mindfulness practice.*

Mindfulness Practice

Mindfulness Helper

Invite today's Mindfulness Helper (MH) to come to the front of the class and sit next to you on a chair.

Prompt the MH to choose another student to turn off the classroom lights.

Prompt the MH to say: "Let's get into our mindful bodies. Close your eyes or look down into your lap. Let's take three deep breaths."

Cue students choose a mindful breathing practice. Possibilities include Gravity Hands, Take Five, Four Square, and Clench and Release.

Say: *Now let's take one more deep breath in and out. Let's listen to the sound mindfully and open your eyes or look up when you can't hear it anymore.*

Ask the MH to ring the bell.

Ask the MH to choose a classmate to turn the lights on.

Ask the MH to return to his or her seat.

Lesson: *Rosie's Brain*

1. **Read** *Rosie's Brain*.

Reflect and Discuss

You might use these questions to shape a discussion:

- What did Rosie notice about her body after she stomped upstairs to her room? (breathing hard, hot face, hands in little balls)
- What part of Rosie's brain was in charge at first? (Amy / The Amygdala)
- How did Rosie respond to her problem with Amy in charge?
- What is the name of the part of the brain that Miss. Pickles represented? (hippocampus)
- What did Miss Pickles take care of for Rosie? (storing memories)
- What did PFC take care of for Rosie? (thinking things over and making good decisions)
- How did Rosie put PFC back in charge, instead of Amy? (taking deep breaths)
- How did Rosie solve her problem when PFC was in charge?

Activity: The Walk, Stop, Wiggle, Sit Game

Say: In *Rosie's Brain*, Rosie used Take Five Breathing to calm her amygdala and put the PFC back in charge. The better we get at putting the PFC back in charge when we need to, the more we'll be able to make good decisions when it really counts.

Here is a new brain game that challenges our prefrontal cortex to focus on one thing intently, ignoring distractions. It gets us out of one way of thinking and challenges us to be more flexible and responsive. It also gets us moving.

Here's how to play. There are many levels of this game.

Give directions:

- We're going to play the game silently so that everyone can hear the directions.
- Make sure that you are not talking and that you are not touching each other.

Level 1: When I say Walk, you walk. When I say Stop, you Stop. When I say Wiggle, you wiggle. When I say Sit, you sit. Got it?

Level 2: This time Walk = Stop
Stop = Walk
Wiggle = Wiggle
Sit = Sit

Level 3: This time: Walk = Stop
Stop = Walk
Wiggle = Sit
Sit = Wiggle

Level 4: This time: Walk = Wiggle
Wiggle = Walk
Sit = Stop
Stop = Sit

You can keep going, changing up the commands or add in new ones. It's pretty hard!

Ask: *How did this feel to you? Was it hard or easy?*

Kindness Pals

Kindness Pal Activity: You can include some or all of the following as time allows, but definitely assign new Kindness Pals.

- Share kind acts from the previous week.
- Assign new Kindness Pals.
- Do the Kindness Pal Challenge (see Week 4)
- Share what you learned about your Kindness Pal with the group.

Closing words: *Okay our time is up for today. Thank you for a great class, everyone. Let's have a nice quiet moment for the bell. If you want to, you can close your eyes, picture your new Kindness Pal, and imagine yourself doing something kind for them this week.*

Ring the bell.

Extensions

Writing Prompts:

Write about a time you found yourself in a situation like Rosie

How did you respond? How could mindfulness have helped?

What are some of the kind things you could do for your Kindness Pal this week?

At Home:

Practice Take Five breathing sometime this week when you feel like your amygdala might be taking over in a situation where it would be better to stay calm.

Week 18
Brain Review

OBJECTIVES: Deepen understanding of how three parts of our brain, the amygdala, the hippocampus, and the prefrontal cortex, operate in regulating our emotions and reactions to stimuli

Practice using real-life scenarios

Practice kindness

PREPARE: A bell or chime

Your Kindness Pals list and Talking Object

Video of **Dr. Daniel Siegel's Hand Model** of the Brain. Watch this before class if you didn't teach this last year or if you need a refresher. This detailed video is for the teacher, **not the students:** Dr. Dan Siegel's *Hand Model of the Brain.* Found at https://www.youtube.com/watch?v=f-m2YcdMdFw. © 2017 Mind Your Brain, Inc. Used with permission. All rights reserved.

Diagram of the Brain (found in Materials for Lessons Section)

Your Kindness Pals list and talking object

Optional: Brainy the Puppet

Rosie's Brain offered a review of the three key parts of the brain last week. This week we offer a deeper dive into how the amygdala, hippocampus and prefrontal cortex work together to help us. We offer more detail on each part of the brain, and encourage students to be curious about how their own individual brains work.

You might like to use the (optional) Brainy the Puppet to illustrate the hand model of the brain. Or, you might choose to use hip-hop artist JusTme's video "Don't Flip yo' Lid" from last year to reinforce this lesson. Find it on JustMindfulness.com.

Introduction

You might say:

Our brain is a very complex part of our bodies, and scientists are constantly learning more about how our brains work. The amygdala, the hippocampus and the prefrontal cortex work together with many other parts of our brains to help you react and respond to situations. We focus on these parts of the brain because of the important roles scientists tell us they play in our fight/flight/freeze response and in our ability to make good decisions.

As you get older, you can continue learning about how your brain works by reading and researching on your own.

Today we are going to look at some scenarios and think about how your brain is working in each one.

Our brains do not all work in the same way. Our classes on the brain are for you to get to know your **own** brain - how do you, personally, respond in a certain situation? Your response may be different from someone else's. What works best for you to calm your amygdala and get your PFC back in charge? Be curious. Use this class to find out more about how your own brain works.

Mindfulness Practice

Invite today's Mindfulness Helper (MH) to come to the front of the class to sit next to you on a chair.

Prompt the MH to choose another student to turn off the classroom lights.

Prompt the MH to say: "Let's get into our mindful bodies. Close your eyes or look down into your lap. Let's take five deep breaths."

Invite students to choose a practice like Take Five, Four Square Breathing, Clench and Release or Gravity Hands.

After a few moments, say: Now let's take one more deep breath in and out. Let's listen to the sound mindfully and open your eyes or look up when you can't hear it anymore.

Ask the MH to ring the bell.

Ask the MH to choose a classmate to turn the lights on**.**

Ask the MH to return to his or her seat.

Lesson: The amygdala, the hippocampus and the prefrontal cortex

1. **A few scenarios**

   Say: *Can you think of a time recently when you got angry? Maybe you were supposed to go to a party and then your parents told you that you couldn't go because you had to babysit for your little sister. Or you tried out for the basketball team and didn't make it. We're going to talk through a few scenarios along those lines.*

   Go over each scenario and have students share out how they would feel and how they would typically react. For each scenario, ask:

   - How do you feel? Write the names of the emotions on the board.
   - How would you handle that?
   - How does that usually work out for you?

   Take a few responses for each scenario.

   Scenarios:

   1. You were invited to a party but you can't go because you have to babysit for your little sister.
   2. You tried out for the basketball team and didn't make it.
   3. You're on the basketball team but you're almost always sitting on the bench during games.
   4. Your friends are all going to a concert but you can't afford the ticket.
   5. Your best friend got the sneakers you wanted but your parents won't get them for you.
   6. You see on social media that your friend had a party and didn't invite you.
   7. You auditioned for a solo in the choir concert and didn't get it.
   8. You finished your ELA paper but you left it at home and you're going to be marked down for lateness.
   9. Ask the class for others - make them very brief.

Say: *These are challenging situations. It can help to understand what is happening in your brain when these things happen.*

2. **The Amygdala, the Hippocampus and the PFC**

   Say: *Let's review and add to what we have learned about our brains.*

   Hold up your hand in the shape of the hand model, or use Brainy the Puppet here.

   Can you do this with your hand? Tuck your thumb inside and then fold your fingers over your thumb. Now your hand looks a little bit like your brain.

   Hold your hand up next to your head.

   The first part is the Amygdala.

   Lift your fingers to show the tucked-in thumb.

   The amygdala is the little almond-shaped part of your brain inside here. Really, the amygdala has two parts, one for each side of the brain, but as we only have one thumb on each hand, we'll just represent it with one thumb.

   The amygdala is an important part of the limbic system, the part of your brain that reacts to things and helps you to feel emotions and remember things. The limbic system is the part of the human brain that developed first.

   Ask: *Who remembers what the amygdala does?*

   Take a few answers.

   Say: *Yes, the amygdala works to protect us. It is a part of the brain that is responsible for helping us feel and respond to emotions, including fear. The amygdala plays a role in our fight/flight/freeze response.*

   Ask: *Is the amygdala helpful in our day-to-day lives?*

   Take a few answers.

   That's right. Yes, but not always. The fight or flight reflex helps to keep us safe when we are in danger. But sometimes it can overreact.

   For example, if you are playing basketball and somebody comes up and takes your ball, your amygdala might tell you to say "Hey give it back!! It's mine!!" Your amygdala's fight reflex is kicking in, and it wants you to grab the ball back.

   Ask: *Can you think of a time when your amygdala told you to do or say something like that?*

   Take a few answers.

Your amygdala makes you feel scared sometimes too. Your amygdala might tell you not to jump off the diving board or not to raise your hand in class to answer a hard question. Your amygdala might tell you not to try out for the travel soccer team or for a solo in a concert. In all of these cases, it's telling you to choose the "flight" option. Run away! But is not getting the solo in the concert the same thing as getting eaten by a saber tooth tiger? Nope. But your amygdala can't always tell the difference.

Ask: *Can you think of a time when your amygdala was trying to protect you from something?*

Take a few answers.

Your amygdala wants to take care of you, to protect you. But if we only listened to our amygdala, we wouldn't be very happy. We'd be in fights with people all of the time, or we wouldn't do anything that we are scared to do, even really fun things like learning how to ride a bike or learning how to dive.

The Prefrontal Cortex (PFC)

Your amygdala wants to keep you safe. But humans have evolved to keep up with the changing world and our brains have evolved too. We developed a new, very important part of our brains called the Prefrontal Cortex.

Fold your fingers back down.

*This part (***pointing to your folded-over fingers***) is called the Prefrontal Cortex. You can call it the PFC for short.*

Ask: *Do you remember what the PFC does?* **Take a few responses.**

That's right. *Your PFC is the part of your brain that helps you to make good decisions. The Prefrontal cortex can calm the activity in the amygdala, and help you to make more thoughtful decisions. It helps you think things over and imagines what will happen.*

The Hippocampus

Finally, we are going to review one more important part of the brain. Who can remember what it is? That's right, the hippocampus!

In fact, your hippocampus helped you to remember the word hippocampus! The hippocampus is like a librarian inside of your brain. It is the part of the brain that stores all of your memories and helps you to retrieve them.

The hippocampus is also part of the limbic system, like the amygdala. There are actually two parts of the hippocampus (or hippocampi), one on each side of the brain, very close to the amygdalae. When we talk about the hippocampus, we are talking about both of them.

Can anybody tell me what you had for breakfast today? (**Let someone answer**.)

Well that memory was stored by your hippocampus! Have you ever been to the beach? Eaten a pepper? Touched a snake? (**Let kids raise their hands if they have done any of those things**.)

So when I asked those questions your brains went looking into the memories that your hippocampus had stored for the answer. Some of us found it, but some of us didn't perhaps because the hippocampus hadn't stored it in the first place.

Kindness Pals

Kindness Pal Activity: You can include some or all of the following as time allows, but definitely assign new Kindness Pals.

- Share kind acts from the previous week.
- Assign new Kindness Pals.
- Do the Kindness Pal Challenge (see Week 4).
- Share what you learned about your Kindness Pal with the group.

Closing words: *Okay our time is up for today. Thank you for a great class, everyone. Let's have a nice quiet moment for the bell. If you want to, you can close your eyes, picture your new Kindness Pal, and imagine yourself doing something kind for them this week.*

Ring the bell.

Extensions

Writing Prompts:

Can you think of a time when your amygdala took over? Was it helpful or not? What could you have done to calm your amygdala?

What are some of the kind things you could do for your Kindness Pal this week?

At Home:

Notice when your amygdala might be taking over. Notice whether the amygdala is being helpful (keeping you from getting stung by a bee, for example) or not (you begin to yell at your brother or sister because you are mad).

Show a friend or family member the hand model of the brain.

Week 19
Your Brain and Basketball

OBJECTIVES: Review how three parts of our brain, the hippocampus, the amygdala and the prefrontal cortex, play a role in regulating our emotions and reactions to stimuli

Practice kindness

PREPARE: A bell or chime

Diagram of the brain (found in Materials for Lessons Section)

7 Copies of the skit *Elijah's Brain* found in the **Materials for Lessons** Section

Your Kindness Pals list and Talking Object

In this lesson, we introduce a new skit: *Elijah's Brain*. This skit helps students more deeply understand the roles of the amygdala, hippocampus and prefrontal cortex. By giving students insight into how their brains work, we help them to realize that they have control over their ability to respond to stimuli.

Introduction

Say: *Today we are going to review the roles of amygdala, hippocampus and prefrontal cortex, and then act out a skit called Elijah's Brain.*

But first, as always, we start with our mindfulness practice.

Mindfulness Practice

Invite today's Mindfulness Helper (MH) to come to the front of the class to sit next to you on a chair.

Prompt the MH to choose another student to turn off the classroom lights.

Prompt the MH to say: "Let's get into our mindful bodies. Close your eyes or look down into your lap. Let's take 3 deep breaths."

Invite students to choose a practice like Take Five, Four Square Breathing, Clench and Release or Gravity Hands.

Say: Now let's take one more deep breath in and out. Let's listen to the sound mindfully and open your eyes or look up when you can't hear it anymore.

Ask the MH to ring the bell.

Ask the MH to choose a classmate to turn the lights on.

Ask the MH to return to his or her seat.

Lesson: Using brain knowledge to help manage anger

1. **Flipping Our Lid**

   Say: I am going to share a situation with you and then ask you how you feel.

   Say: Imagine that you are having a play-date with a friend. You have a new game and you can't wait to play. You've been looking forward to playing your new game all day. When your friend arrives she says that she has been cooped up inside all day and can't wait to go out to play soccer.

   Ask the class:

   - How do you feel? (Angry, upset, disappointed.)
   - What does your amygdala tell you to do? (Cry, go to your room, yell, tell her that if you can't play Monopoly, you'll hold your breath until you turn blue…)
   - How will things turn out if you only listen to your amygdala? (Your friend will be mad, you will miss out, she might go home, won't want to play with you anymore…)

   When we feel like that, it's as if we've flipped our lid.

   Flip your fingers up exposing the amygdala.

   It can feel like our amygdala is in charge, and we can't think very well because our Prefrontal Cortex or PFC is no longer in charge. You really need your Prefrontal Cortex (or PFC) to help you work this out. But how can you get it back in charge again?

   When we take our deep breaths and take care of our anger, it helps to bring our Prefrontal Cortex back in charge.

   Fold your fingers down slowly.

   It can take a little while to work, but once we have our lids back on we can think about what we want to do. We have choices.

Putting the PFC Back In Charge

Once you have your lid back on and your PFC is in charge, you can think about how much you like your friend, and you start to think about your options.

Ask: *What are some other ways to solve this problem? (Take turns playing soccer and your game, let your guest decide what to play, and so on.)*

Say: *Do you see how your PFC helps you see that you have choices and sometimes what your amygdala wants you to do isn't always the best idea?*

The next time you get angry, see if you can remember that this is your amygdala talking to you. See if you can use your breathing to help take care of your amygdala.

It's important to remember that your amygdala is trying to take care of you. If you feel angry or upset that is fine. All of your emotions are fine.

The problem with anger is that sometimes the way we express it can make things worse for us and for those around us.

Once you have calmed down, you can figure out the best way to express what is bothering you so that you can take care of it.

We are not trying to get rid of our anger or any of our emotions. We're just trying to make sure that our feelings aren't controlling us.

2. **Skit: Elijah's Brain**

    Invite 4 volunteers to participate and assign them roles: Elijah, his amygdala, his hippocampus, and his prefrontal cortex.

    Pass out a script to each actor and have the kids act out the skit.

    Invite the audience to notice what they feel in their bodies as they watch the skit. They can also use their hands to model "flipping your lid" and "bringing your lid back down" along with the characters in the play.

Reflect and Discuss

You might use these questions to shape a discussion:

- Why did Elijah's amygdala decide to take over?
- What was Amygdala's plan for Elijah?
- How would things have turned out if Elijah had let his amygdala take over?

- Why did the Amygdala suggest that Elijah either stand still, throw the ball hard, or run away? (The fight, flight or freeze reflex)
- How did the Hippocampus and PFC help Elijah to make the shot?
- Can you think about what kinds of things might be upsetting or distracting during a basketball game?
- How could mindfulness and what you know about your brain help play better?

Kindness Pals

Kindness Pal Activity: You can include some or all of the following as time allows, but definitely assign new Kindness Pals.

- Share kind acts from the previous week.
- Assign new Kindness Pals.
- Do the Kindness Pal Challenge (see Week 4).
- Share what you learned about your Kindness Pal with the group.

Closing words: *Okay our time is up for today. Thank you for a great class, everyone. Let's have a nice quiet moment for the bell. If you want to, you can close your eyes, picture your new Kindness Pal, and imagine yourself doing something kind for them this week.*

Ring the bell.

Extensions

Writing Prompts:

Have you ever had an experience like Elijah's? Write about it.

What are some kind things you could do for your Kindness Pal this week?

At Home:

Notice times when you think your amygdala might be guiding your actions, and notice other times when your PFC might be more in charge.

Unit 6
Conflict Resolution

Week 20
Conflict Escalator: Swings are for Babies

OBJECTIVES: Review the concept of a **Conflict Escalator** (developed and named by William Kreidler)

Help children understand how and why conflicts get worse

Practice kindness

PREPARE: A bell or chime

6 copies of the *Swings are for Babies* Skit found in the **Materials for Lessons** Section.

Your Kindness Pals list and Talking Object

We are now entering the section we have called "Conflict Resolution." In fact, everything you have been teaching until this point has laid the critical foundation for this work. Practicing mindfulness and kindness and understanding how our brains work as part of conflict resolution raise the chances that differences can be resolved peacefully and constructively.

In this lesson, you will review the concept of a Conflict Escalator, developed and named by educator William Kreidler. This metaphor helps children understand how and why conflicts get worse. This is a key step in learning how to de-escalate conflicts and how to control behavior in conflict situations. You will also have a chance here to review The Conflict Toolbox and the very important Conflict CAT through the skit.

Introduction

Say: *Today we will be exploring tools for solving conflicts, and then we will have the chance to practice using them in a new skit.*

But first, our Mindfulness practice.

Mindfulness Practice

Say: *Today for our Mindfulness practice I am going to ask you to choose which practice you would like to do. Since we're going to be working on conflicts today* *let's think about which of our Mindfulness practices would help you to calm down when you are in a conflict.*

Ask *for some suggestions.*

Say: *Those are great suggestions. Today I'd like you to choose Take Five, Four Square, Gravity Hands or Clench and Release.*

Ask *for a student to demonstrate each one.*

Say: *Okay now let's have our Mindful Moment. Remember, when the Mindfulness Helper says "Let's take some deep breaths," you can decide which practice you want to do today.*

Invite today's Mindfulness Helper (MH) to come to the front of the class to sit next to you on a chair.

Prompt the MH to choose another student to turn off the classroom lights.

Prompt the MH to say: "Let's get into our mindful bodies. Close your eyes or look down into your lap. Let's take some deep breaths."

Say: *Now let's take one more deep breath in and out. Let's listen to the sound mindfully and open your eyes or look up when you can't hear it anymore.*

Ask the MH to ring the bell when the mindful breathing is complete.

Ask the MH to choose a classmate to turn the lights on.

Ask the MH to return to his or her seat.

Lesson: The Conflict Escalator

1. What is the Conflict Escalator?

You might say:

One way to *think about how conflicts get bigger is called the Conflict Escalator.*

Draw an escalator on the board. See the Materials for Lessons Section for blank escalator that you may fill in. Refer to image at the end of this lesson for an example. For this activity, make sure that the Conflict Escalator you draw has six steps before it reaches the top.

Ask the children to describe what an escalator does.

Explain that when conflict gets worse, we say that the people involved are going up the Conflict Escalator. (**or invite a student to explain**). Each step represents something that someone did or said that made the conflict escalate or get bigger.

Ask: *What is always at the top of the Conflict Escalator?*

    A. Trouble

2. **Skit: Swings are For Babies**

    Say: *We have a skit today called "Swings are for Babies" that will help us experience what it's like to go up and down the conflict escalator. I will need 6 volunteers to act out the skit.*

    Ask for 6 volunteers to act out the skit. The characters are Dakota, Derrick, Dawson, Mateo, Zion, and Tamera. Hand them each a copy of the script.

    Remind those not in the skit that the audience plays an active role. They can notice where they are feeling emotions in their bodies as the skit unfolds.

    You might also invite audience members to point a finger upward when the actors are going up the conflict escalator, and downward when they are making progress toward solving the conflict constructively.

    Act out the skit.

Reflect and Discuss

Say: *Okay now let's map the conflict from the skit on the Conflict Escalator.*

For this activity you can find a variety of ways to engage your students in the activity.

- Draw the conflict escalator on your board, and use sticky notes to represent each person who escalates / de-escalates the conflict. As one person does something to change the conflict, have a student come up and move that person's sticky note up/down the conflict escalator.

- If you have a white board in your room, draw the conflict escalator on your white board and then use different color magnets to represent the different people in the conflict. As one person does something to escalate the conflict, have a student come up and move that person's magnet up a step.

- You could also use different color markers and have students draw a dot or that character's initial, or use sticky notes, or even go three-dimensional and use blocks to build a conflict escalator and other small objects to represent the people. Use what you have available and your imagination!

Ask: the following questions:

Who can remember what this conflict was about?

- The kids were disagreeing about what to do at the park - play basketball or go on the swings. (Write that at the bottom of the escalator.)

Who sent the conflict up the Conflict Escalator? What did somebody say that made this conflict escalate?

- Dawson said, "Swings are for babies."

Have someone "put" Dawson on the conflict escalator.

Then what happened, what was the next thing that caused the conflict to escalate?

- Dawson said "Everybody knows that basketball is cooler than the swings."

Have someone move Dawson up the conflict escalator.

Why did that cause the conflict to escalate?

- Because the other kids were trying to point out to him that both activities were fun but he kept going making judgments about what the other kids wanted to do.

Then what happened to make the conflict escalate?

- Dakota said: All you care about is being cool, Dawson. You too, Derrick!

Have someone put Dakota on the next step of the conflict escalator. Keep going until you get to Mateo.

Who stops the conflict from escalating?

- Mateo

What does he say?

Take answers and begin to show how the kids were able to de-escalate the conflict and bring it down the Conflict Escalator.

Say: *Great job! Okay we'll work more on this next time.*

Kindness Pals

Kindness Pal Activity: You can include some or all of the following as time allows, but definitely assign new Kindness Pals.

- Share kind acts from the previous week.
- Assign new Kindness Pals.
- Do the Kindness Pal Challenge (see Week 4).
- Share what you learned about your Kindness Pal with the group.

Closing words: *Okay our time is up for today. Thank you for a great class, everyone. Let's have a nice quiet moment for the bell. If you want to, you can close your eyes, picture your new Kindness Pal, and imagine yourself doing something kind for them this week.*

Ring the bell.

Extensions

Writing Prompts:

Describe a time when you have gone up the conflict escalator. How did you come down?

What are some of the kind things you could do for your Kindness Pal this week?

At Home:

Practice two different mindfulness practices this week. Which one helps you most?

Teach a family member or friend one of our mindfulness practices and explain to them how it might help them.

Week 21
MOFL: Apology Practice

OBJECTIVES: Understand what makes a good apology

Practice apologizing

Practice kindness

PREPARE: A bell or chime

Your Kindness Pals list and Talking Object

Copies of worksheets: Apology Practice 1 and 2 from the **Materials for Lessons** Section for each pair.

A critical component of successful, peaceful conflict resolution is a good apology. Apologizing can be challenging and takes practice. When we start with mindfulness to calm anger, apologizing is more accessible. In this lesson we explore the four components of a good apology: Mean it, Own it, Fix it and then Let it Go.

Introduction

You might say: *Today we are going to focus on apologizing. Apologizing is an important part of working out conflicts. If you have gone up the Conflict Escalator, then you have most likely done or said something that you need to apologize for. Today we are going to be thinking about what makes a good apology.*

Mindfulness Practice

Invite today's Mindfulness Helper (MH) to come to the front of the class to sit next to you on a chair.

Prompt the MH to choose another student to turn off the classroom lights.

Prompt the MH to say: "Let's get into our mindful bodies. Close your eyes or look down into your lap. Let's take 3 deep breaths."

You might say: *Today I'm going to be describing some situations and I want you to try to imagine that they are happening to you. Try to notice what you feel and if you can try to notice where you feel it in your body.*

Let's imagine…

You are bringing home an art project and someone bumps into you and knocks it out of your hands. It falls on the floor and breaks into pieces…

Ask: How do you feel? Where do you feel it?

You are bringing home an art project and someone bumps into you and knocks it out of your hands. The person turns around and says "Sorry!" and runs off.

Ask: How do you feel? Where do you feel it?

You are bringing home an art project and someone bumps into you and knocks it out of your hands. The person turns around and sees what happened. They say "Oh my gosh I'm so sorry! I broke your project! Can I help you put it back together?

Ask: How do you feel? Where do you feel it?

Okay now let's think about this:

You borrowed a book from a friend and you accidentally spilled chocolate milk on some of the pages.

Ask: How do you feel? Where do you feel it?

You wait for it to dry and you give it back to your friend and don't tell them about the milk.

Ask: How do you feel? Where do you feel it?

You borrowed a book from a friend and you accidentally spilled chocolate milk on some of the pages. You give it back to your friend and say "Chocolate milk spilled on your book. Sorry!"

Ask: How do you feel? Where do you feel it?

You borrowed a book from a friend and you accidentally spilled chocolate milk on some of the pages. You give them the book back and say "I spilled chocolate milk on your book. I'm really sorry! I will save up my money to get you a new one. I'm really sorry.

Ask: How do you feel? Where do you feel it?

Pause

Say: *Now let's take one more deep breath in and out. Let's listen to the sound mindfully and open your eyes or look up when you can't hear it anymore.*

Ask the MH to ring the bell when the mindful breathing is complete.

Ask the MH to choose a classmate to turn the lights on**.**

Ask the MH to return to his or her seat.

Reflect and Discuss

Go over each scenario and ask kids to share how they were feeling.

Lesson: What makes a good apology?

1. **MOFL Role Play**

   To explain what Mean it, Own it, Fix it, Let it go (MOFL) means, try using this skit-based approach.

   Choose a student to act with you.

   Invite the student to sit at a desk and draw.

   Walk over and bump the student while she is drawing so she messes up.

   Prompt the student to say: "Hey! You messed up my drawing!"

   Act out these four apology scenarios:

   1. You say, "Sorry!" and keep walking.

   Ask: Is that a good apology? Why or why not? **Take a few answers**.

   2. Act it out again but this time say "Sorry! I needed to get by" and keep walking.

   Ask: Is that a good apology? Why or why not? **Take a few answers**.

   3. Act it out again but this time say "Oh no! I'm so sorry! I wasn't watching where I was going. Can I help you fix it? I'm really sorry."

   Ask: Is that a good apology? Why or why not? **Take a few answers.**

   4. **Act it out again** but this time say "Oh no! I'm so sorry! I wasn't watching where I was going. Can I help you fix it? I'm really sorry. Do you forgive me? You have to forgive me! I said I was sorry! Tell me that it's okay!"

   Ask: Is that a good apology? Why or why not? **Take a few answers.**

2. **What is MOFL?**

   Now write on the board **M O F L.**

   Ask if anyone can guess what the letters stand for. Give them the hint that it has something to do with apologizing.

   Explain that the **M stands for Mean it**. A good apology has to be sincere and the person receiving it should see that you are truly sorry.

Ask: *Why wasn't the apology: "Chocolate milk spilled on your book. Sorry." good?*

Somebody will probably say because the person didn't take responsibility for what they did. The **O in MOFL stands for Own it.** You have to take responsibility for what you did. Rather than saying "Mistakes were made" we would say "I made a mistake."

Ask: *When your art project was broken and the person apologized and offered to try to put it back together what were they doing?* (trying to fix it)

The **F stands for Fix it.** Even though it's not always possible, it's important to try to make amends and see if there is anything you can do to fix or remedy the situation.

Ask: *Was the fourth apology a good one? Why or why not?*

The **L stands for Let it Go**. Sometimes when people apologize they get very upset if the person receiving their apology doesn't accept it. It's important to remember that sometimes people aren't ready to forgive. Maybe they are still upset about what happened, even if they aren't really mad at you. We need to offer apologies and then let it go and let the person come to forgiveness when and if they are ready.

Ask: *So, what are the four important parts of a good apology?*

Mean it, Own it, Fix it, Let it go = MOFL.

Mean it - show the person that you really regret what happened. Ask for an example.

Own it - in the meditation one apology was "Milk spilled on your book." Is that showing that you take responsibility for your actions? Do you have to take responsibility even if it was an accident? Ask for an example.

Fix it - what can you do to make things right? Ask for an example.

Let it go - don't chase the person around making them forgive you. Sometimes that takes time - that isn't what this is about. This is about you offering something to the other person. You can't make them take it. But you do the right thing anyway. The only person you can control is yourself. Ask for an example.

3. **Apology Review**

   You might say: *Today you're going to work with your Kindness Pal to review some apologies.*

   Assign the new Kindness Pals.

   Give one copy of each worksheet to each Kindness Pal pair.

Instruct: *Take your time to read them out loud and then check off whether you think the apology shows that the person Means it, Owns it, tries to Fix it, and Lets it Go. Then circle the best apology.*

Ask students to complete both worksheets as described above.

Bring the group back together after about 5 minutes.

Reflect and Discuss:

- What are the pros and cons of each apology in terms of MOFL?
- What do you think are the best apologies and why. You could ask: "MOFL or Awful?"

Kindness Pals

Kindness Pal Activity: You can include some or all of the following as time allows.

- Share kind acts from the previous week.
- Do the Kindness Pal Challenge (see Week 4).
- Share what you learned about your Kindness Pal with the group.

Closing words: *Okay our time is up for today. Thank you for a great class, everyone. Let's have a nice quiet moment for the bell. If you want to, you can close your eyes, picture your new Kindness Pal, and imagine yourself doing something kind for them this week.*

Ring the bell.

Extensions

Writing Prompts:

Can you think of a time when you received a good apology from someone? When you made a good apology to someone else?

What are some of the kind things you could do for your Kindness Pal this week?

At Home:

Practice two different mindfulness practices this week. Which one helps you most?

Teach a family member or friend one of our mindfulness practices and explain to them how it might help them.

Week 22
Conflict Toolbox Matching Game

OBJECTIVES: Practice with the Conflict CAT

Practice kindness

PREPARE: A bell or chime

Copies of the Toolbox Matching Game worksheet for each pair from the **Materials for Lessons** Section

Your Kindness Pals list and Talking Object

In the Swings are for Babies skit, the children modeled using the Conflict CAT, though you haven't directly taught it yet. Today you'll (re-) introduce the CAT, which encompasses the three critical steps to solving any conflict productively:

C - Calm down using mindfulness techniques that help us become aware of what we are feeling, and then to manage those feelings using mindful breathing or other mindfulness skills to allow the PFC to take control from the amygdala.

A – Apologize using skills taught in the last lesson.

T - Toolbox. In this lesson, we focus primarily on the tools children can practice using to solve conflicts, and we introduce a new game. These tools are most effective after the first two steps have been taken!

Introduction

Say: *From our very first class, we have been learning about conflict resolution - even though that's not what we called it. In our mindfulness lessons, we've learned many ways to help us to calm down when we are angry. Calming down is the first step to solving a disagreement.*

We've also learned about what happens in our brains when we get angry, how we flip our lids and we let our amygdala take over. This helps us understand how mindfulness is useful in a conflict - it assists in putting the PFC back in charge.

We have learned about empathy - trying to see a situation from someone else's point of view. And we've been practicing kindness every class.

In Swings are for Babies, we learned about what conflict is, and how it escalates or goes up the Conflict Escalator.

We've learned about the important skill of apologizing, and we practiced this skill in several of the skits we've acted out.

This is all really powerful information that most people, including many grown-ups, don't have. With these tools we can make our own lives easier and make the world a more peaceful place.

Today we are going to be focusing on helpful tools for solving conflicts. You can use these tools without using mindfulness and apologizing first, but they don't work nearly as well.

Mindfulness Practice

Invite today's Mindfulness Helper (MH) to come to the front of the class to sit next to you on a chair.

Prompt the MH to choose another student to turn off the classroom lights.

Prompt the MH to say: "Let's get into our mindful bodies. Close your eyes or look down into your lap. Let's take some deep breaths."

Say: *Choose the mindfulness practice you want to do: Take Five, Gravity Hands, Clench and Release, Four Square, even See, Hear, Feel.*

After a few moments, say: *Now let's take one more deep breath in and out. Let's listen to the sound mindfully and open your eyes or look up when you can't hear it anymore.*

Signal the MH to ring the bell.

Ask the MH to choose a classmate to turn the lights on.

Turn and Talk

Remind the kids that before they start their chat make sure that everyone has a partner.

Share with someone sitting near you which practice you chose and why. Listen to them sharing with you.

Invite a few students to share what practice they chose and why.

Lesson: The Conflict Toolbox

1. **The Conflict C.A.T.**

   Today we are going to put all of these pieces together in a fun way that is easy to remember.

   If applicable, ask: *Does anyone remember what we called the conflict resolution method we used last year?*

   The Conflict C.A.T. *stands for the three most important things to do to work out a conflict.*

   Ask: *Can anyone tell me what they are?*

   > Calm down
   > Apologize
   > Toolbox

   Ask: *Who can guess or remember the tools in the toolbox?*

   Take some answers and write them on the board until you have the following.

   Discuss each one for a few minutes, and ask for examples of how students have used them.

   > **Taking Turns** - take turns using the object.
   >
   > **Sharing** - share it.
   >
   > **Being Kind** - let the other person have their way.
   >
   > **Leave it to Chance** - flip a coin, rock, paper, scissors, etc.
   >
   > **Compromise** - if you are arguing over what kind of pizza to have maybe you decide to eat pasta instead as long as you both like pasta.
   >
   > **Pause the Conflict** - if you are too angry to work things out take a while to calm down and then come back to working things out.
   >
   > **Skip the Conflict** - sometimes whatever you are having a conflict about isn't worth it going up the Conflict Escalator over. Or maybe you are trying to calm down and work things out but the other person keeps escalating. Sometimes you can just decide to walk away and skip the conflict because that is what is best for you.
   >
   > **Get Help** - ask someone else to help you to work things out.

2. **Choose one of the activities that follow, or do both if time permits.**

   ### The Matching Game

   Explain: *Each of these tools has a symbol to go with it. Today you're going to work with your Kindness Pal to see if you can figure out which symbol goes with which tool in the toolbox. Some of them are kind of obvious and some are a little tricky. You're going to draw a line between the matches.*

   Hand out one worksheet for each pair. Give them a few minutes to complete it.

   Bring the class back together and have them share their answers.

   Say: Now we're going to think about how we can use these tools.

   ### Scenarios

   You might say: *I'm going to describe a conflict, and I want you to tell me which tool would work the best and why.*

   Suggest these situations and ask which tools the class would use. Take a few answers for each one and discuss.

   - You and your friend both want to go first in a game.
   - You and a classmate both want to sit in the class rocking chair.
   - You want to draw but somebody is already using all of the markers.
   - You and a friend can't agree on a movie to watch.
   - You and your sister are doing homework and you both need to use the family computer.

   Please feel free to come up with your own situations that reflect the needs of your class.

Kindness Pals

   Kindness Pal Activity: You can include some or all of the following as time allows.

   - Share kind acts from the previous week.
   - Assign new Kindness Pals.
   - Do the Kindness Pal Challenge (see Week 4).
   - Share what you learned about your Kindness Pal with the group.

Closing words: *Okay our time is up for today. Thank you for a great class, everyone. Let's have a nice quiet moment for the bell. If you want to, you can close your eyes, picture your new Kindness Pal, and imagine yourself doing something kind for them this week.*

Ring the bell.

Extensions

Writing Prompts:

Can you think of a time when you used one or more of the tools from the Toolbox?

Did you use the first two steps - Calm Down and Apologize - first? If you didn't, how might that have helped?

What are some kind things you could do for your Kindness Pal this week?

At Home:

Notice: is there one tool from the Conflict Toolbox that you find yourself using most often?

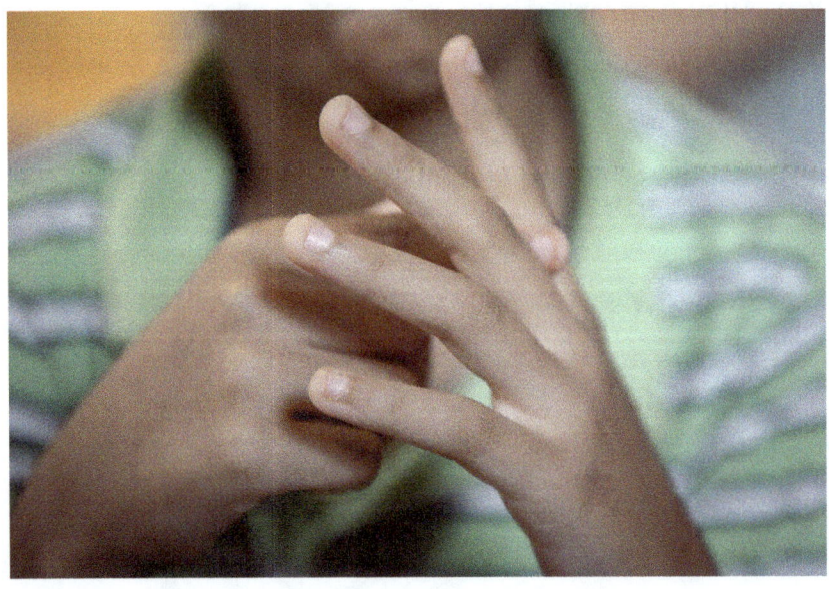

Week 23
Conflict C.A.T. Role Play

OBJECTIVES: Practice the Conflict Resolution skills taught in previous lessons

Practice kindness

PREPARE: A bell or chime

Copy "Conflict C.A.T. Role Play Scenarios" (at end of lesson) and cut into strips. Alternatively, you may write your own conflicts on slips of paper or index cards to meet the specific needs of your classroom.

Have a poster of the Conflict Escalator, the Conflict C.A.T., and the Toolbox up where the kids can see them. See Materials for Lessons Section.

Your Kindness Pals list and talking object

Now that you have introduced and reviewed the three components of the Conflict C.A.T., the students are ready to put it to work. The more students practice using these tools when they are not really necessary - i.e., through skits and role plays - the more likely it is that they will be able to call on them when they are really needed. Your students might notice that this lesson is similar to the lesson in Week 22 of the Peace of Mind Core Curriculum for Grades 3-5 - it bears repeating.

Introduction

Say: *So we've learned a lot about working out conflicts so far. We've learned about how to use our breathing to help us to Calm Down. We've practiced apologizing in the skits that we've acted out. We've learned eight tools to use to work out conflicts. For today's challenge, let's see if we can put it all together.*

Mindfulness Practice

Invite today's Mindfulness Helper (MH) to come to the front of the class to sit next to you on a chair.

Prompt the MH to choose another student to turn off the classroom lights.

Prompt the MH to say: "Let's get into our mindful bodies. Close your eyes or look down into your lap. Let's take some deep breaths."

Say: *Choose the mindfulness practice you want to do.*

Say: *Now let's take one more deep breath in and out. Let's listen to the sound mindfully and open your eyes or look up when you can't hear it anymore.*

Signal the MH to ring the bell.

Ask the MH to choose a classmate to turn the lights on.

Ask the MH to return to his or her seat.

Lesson: Conflict Resolution Practice

1. **Explain the Conflict C.A.T. Role Play**

   You might say:

   Today I'm going to ask you to work with your new Kindness Pal.

   I am going to give each of you a conflict to work out in a role-play. You'll have a few minutes to work out how you are going to do it and to think about which tool you are going to use. Make sure that your role-play shows all the parts of the Conflict C.A.T.

   You can show us how you go up the Conflict Escalator a little bit (**this is fun**), *but then we want to see how you come down.*

   One of you has to say: "Uh oh, we're going up the Conflict Escalator." You have to show that you are taking some deep breaths. At least one of you has to apologize.

   Then you need to show us that you are using one of the tools in the Toolbox.

   Emphasize: *The rules are: no bad language and no touching each other. Agreed?*

   When time is up, I'll choose some pairs to come up and show us what you've done.

2. **Conflict Resolution Role Play**

   Assign new Kindness Pals so that they can work together on this activity.

   Pass out the conflict scenarios when everyone is paired up.

Ring a bell to begin. Students begin to work out scenarios using the Conflict CAT.

Ring the bell again when time is up. Be flexible with the time.

> *NOTE:* **The real learning is coming from this part of the process so don't rush it.**

3. Share

Invite a few pairs to come up and show the class what they've come up with.

Make sure that they have covered all of the Conflict C.A.T. steps.

Kindness Pals

Kindness Pal Activity: You can include some or all of the following as time allows.

- Share kind acts from the previous week.
- Do the Kindness Pal Challenge (see Week 4).
- Share what you learned about your Kindness Pal with the group.

Closing words: *Okay our time is up for today. Thank you for a great class, everyone. Let's have a nice quiet moment for the bell. If you want to, you can close your eyes, picture your new Kindness Pal, and imagine yourself doing something kind for them this week.*

Ring the bell.

Extensions

Writing Prompts:

Describe another scenario from your own life when you might have been able to use the Conflict C.A.T. to resolve a conflict.

In your opinion, is one part of the Conflict C.A.T. more important than the others?

What are some kind things you could do for your Kindness Pal this week?

At Home:

If you find yourself in a conflict, practice using the Conflict C.A.T. this week.

Conflict C.A.T. Role Play Scenarios
Copy and cut apart to hand to your students.

Two kids are arguing about what to name the class pet.

Two kids disagree about what movie to go see.

Two kids argue over whether to play basketball or play four square during recess.

Two kids argue over what kind of ice cream to get.

Two kids argue about whether pizza or tacos are better.

Two kids argue over whose turn it is to sit by the window in the car.

Two kids argue about who gets to use the family computer.

Two kids argue about what to watch on TV.

Two kids argue over who gets to check out a new library book.

Two kids argue over what is the best superhero.

Two kids argue over whether soccer is better than hockey.

Week 24
Create Your Own Scenarios

Objectives: Integrate skills learned over the entire year to solve conflicts skillfully

Practice kindness

Prepare: A bell or chime

Display posters of the Conflict Escalator, the Conflict C.A.T., and the Toolbox where kids can see them (see Materials for Lessons Section)

Your Kindness Pals list and Talking Object

In this lesson, students will create their own conflict and conflict resolution scenarios. Their process should reflect all of the parts of the Conflict C.A.T. and the Conflict Escalator. This type of practice is essential if the students are to develop the ability to use these tools in real situations.

Introduction

Say: *Today we are going to be role-playing again. But this time you are going to create your own conflict scenarios. The reason we are learning about the Conflict C.A.T. is so that you develop these skills for life - not just for school. Today we'll have a chance to think about where you might use the C.A.T. in real situations you have faced with your friends or siblings.*

But first, mindfulness practice. As you'll see, starting with mindfulness practice helps in real life situations, too.

Mindfulness Practice

Invite today's Mindfulness Helper (MH) to come to the front of the class to sit next to you on a chair.

Prompt the MH to choose another student to turn off the classroom lights.

Prompt the MH to say: "Let's get into our mindful bodies. Close your eyes or look down into your lap. Let's take 3 deep breaths."

Invite today's Mindfulness Helper (MH) to come to the front of the class to sit next to you on a chair.

Prompt the MH to choose another student to turn off the classroom lights.

Prompt the MH to say: "Let's get into our mindful bodies. Close your eyes or look down into your lap. Let's take some deep breaths."

Say: *Choose the mindfulness practice you want to do.*

Say: *Now let's take one more deep breath in and out. Let's listen to the sound mindfully and open your eyes or look up when you can't hear it anymore.*

Signal the MH to ring the bell.

Ask the MH to choose a classmate to turn the lights on.

Ask the MH to return to his or her seat.

Lesson: Conflict Resolution Scenarios

1. **Create Skits**

    You might say:

    So, let's create our skits. Just like last time, your skit needs to show all the parts of the Conflict C.A.T. You can show us how you go up the Conflict Escalator a little bit (this is fun), but then we want to see how you come down.

    Here are the rules:

    1. One of you has to say: "Uh oh, we're going up the Conflict Escalator."

    2. You have to show that you are taking some deep breaths, using Take Five, Gravity Hands, Four Square Breathing, Clench and Release or another practice.

    3. At least one of you has to apologize.

    4. Then you need to show us that you are using one of the tools in the Toolbox.

    5. Make sure that your conflict is realistic and appropriate.

    6. The rules are no bad language and no touching each other. Got it?

    When time is up, I'll choose some pairs to come up and show us what you've done.

    Assign new Kindness Pals so that they can work together.

    Walk around and check in with each pair. Key points to emphasize:
    - Make sure that they are role-playing something appropriate and realistic.
    - Ask them what tool they are planning to use.

- Encourage them not to spend much time going up the Conflict Escalator but rather to focus on coming down.

Call a halt when all of the pairs have developed their scenarios.

3. **Share**

   Ask for volunteers to come to the front of the class to act out their scenarios.

   Invite the audience to notice when and why the characters are going up the conflict escalator and how they come down.

Kindness Pals

Kindness Pal Activity: You can include some or all of the following as time allows.

- Share kind acts from the previous week.
- Do the Kindness Pal Challenge (see Week 4)
- Share what you learned about your Kindness Pal with the group.

Closing words: *Okay our time is up for today. Thank you for a great class, everyone. Let's have a nice quiet moment for the bell. If you want to, you can close your eyes, picture your new Kindness Pal, and imagine yourself doing something kind for them this week.*

Ring the bell.

Extensions

Writing Prompts:

Write about a time you used the Conflict C.A.T. outside of class, or a time when you think you could use it.

What are some kind things you could do for your Kindness Pal this week?

At Home:

If you find yourself in a conflict, practice using the Conflict C.A.T. this week. Notice what parts of the CAT are most challenging for you, and what works well.

Explain the C.A.T. to a friend of family member.

Week 25
Conflict C.A.T. Game

OBJECTIVES: Practice the Conflict Resolution skills taught in previous lessons

Practice kindness

PREPARE: A bell or chime

Have a poster of the Conflict Escalator, the Conflict C.A.T., and the Toolbox up where the kids can see them. See Materials for Lessons Section

Conflict CAT Game sets for your whole class (2-8 students per set)

Split up the class into groups of 4-8

Your Kindness Pals list and talking object

As you can tell, we believe that practice, practice, practice is key to successful conflict resolution. The more we practice our skills when they are not really needed, the more prepared we'll be when a real conflict arises.

Today is our culminating Conflict CAT Challenge day. Based on many years of work with students in the classroom, Peace of Mind has developed a game that helps kids work together to put their mindfulness practices, apologizing skills, and conflict resolution tools to work to solve conflicts - and helps teachers see what their students have learned. Not surprisingly, it's called the Conflict CAT Game.

Please note: The Conflict CAT game is really fun and kids enjoy playing it, but buying it is optional. Each game is for 2-8 players. You would need enough sets for your whole class to play at the same time. (You might also just invest in one set to have in your classroom for kids to play at other times.)

If you choose not to purchase the game, you can repeat the lesson from Week 24 having the kids work with a different partner.

Introduction

Say: *So we've learned a lot about working out conflicts so far. We've learned about how to use our breathing to help us to Calm Down. We've practiced*

apologizing in the skits that we've acted out. We've learned eight tools to use to work out conflicts.

Today we're going to play a game that will help us see how skilled we have become at using what we've learned to solve conflicts.

The game is called- The Conflict C.A.T. Game!

Mindfulness Practice

Invite today's Mindfulness Helper (MH) to come to the front of the class to sit next to you on a chair.

Prompt the MH to choose another student to turn off the classroom lights.

Prompt the MH to say: "Let's get into our mindful bodies. Close your eyes or look down into your lap. Let's take some deep breaths."

Say: *Choose the mindfulness practice you want to do.*

Say: *Now let's take one more deep breath in and out. Let's listen to the sound mindfully and open your eyes or look up when you can't hear it anymore.*

Signal the MH to ring the bell.

Ask the MH to choose a classmate to turn the lights on.

Ask the MH to return to his or her seat.

Lesson: The Conflict C.A.T. Game

1. **Apologizing**

   You might say: *Today we are going to play a game that will help us to practice using the Conflict C.A.T. method.*

   Before we start the game we're going to talk about apologizing. In this game you are going to learn how to say "I'm sorry" in a bunch of different languages. Let's go over some of these together before we play.

   > *NOTE: Unless you speak a lot of languages you might want to use Google Translate or another service to pronounce the different languages.*

   Go over each card and have the kids repeat the words a few times.

2. **Rules of the Game**

   Say: *Now let's get started. Here's how you play.*

   > **NOTE:** *You might want to copy these directions and post them in the room. It's easy once they get the hang of it.*

   Conflict C.A.T. Game Directions:

   Number of players per set: 2-8

   Set up:

   1. Separate cards into four piles: Mindfulness, Tools, Conflicts, Apologies
   2. Place the cards face down on a table in four piles.
   3. Decide who will be the first two actors.
   4. Decide who will be the timer.

   Goal: Act out the conflict written on the card and solve the conflict using the mindfulness skill, tool, and apology on the cards you choose.

   What you do:

   1. The timer draws a card from each pile and turns them face up on the table.
   2. The actors take a moment to look at the four cards that the timer has drawn.
   3. The timer sets a timer (or just gets ready to count) to 10 seconds.
   4. Timer says "Action!" and the actors start acting out the conflict - going up the Conflict Escalator.
   5. After ten seconds the Timer says "Time!" and the actors have to start to work out the conflict.
   6. One actor must say: "We're going up the Conflict Escalator!"
   7. Then the actors role play working out the conflict by using the cards they have drawn: they do the mindfulness practice, they choose a language for an apology, and then they try to solve the conflict using one of the tools on the card.

> **NOTE:** *If neither of the tools is an appropriate way to solve the conflict then they can choose another "Tool" card.*

8. Once the conflict is resolved the players switch parts and play again.

If you have more kids you can spread out the jobs like Timer, Card-Drawer, Bell Ringer, etc.

3. Play the Game!

It will be noisy with all of the groups playing at the same time. Walk around and see if it looks like they are following all of the steps. After each group has gone through all of the conflicts, have them clean up the games and come back together as a group.

Reflect and Discuss

Prompt a discussion with these questions:

- How did that go?
- Did you have conflicts within your group while you were playing the Conflict C.A.T. game?
- Were you able to work out those conflicts?
- Did you enjoy learning how to say "I'm Sorry" in different languages?
- Does anybody remember how to say "I'm Sorry" in a different language?
- Does anybody want to share how to say "I'm sorry" in a language that we didn't cover?

Say: *You now have skills that most people don't have. I hope that you will really try to start using these skills in your real life. Using these skills is pretty easy here in class but a lot more challenging when you are really angry.*

If everyone in our world knew how to work out conflicts like this, our world would be a much more peaceful place. I hope that you will use what you have learned so far in Peace Class to make your corner of the world more peaceful.

Kindness Pals

Kindness Pal Activity: You can include some or all of the following as time allows, but do assign new Kindness Pals.

- Share kind acts from the previous week.
- Assign new Kindness Pals.
- Do the Kindness Pal Challenge (see Week 4).
- Share what you learned about your Kindness Pal with the group.

Closing words: *Okay our time is up for today. Thank you for a great class, everyone. Let's have a nice quiet moment for the bell. If you want to, you can close your eyes, picture your new Kindness Pal, and imagine yourself doing something kind for them this week.*

Ring the bell.

Extensions

Writing Prompts:

Write about a time you used the Conflict C.A.T. outside of class, or a time when you think you could have used it.

What's the hardest part of the Conflict C.A.T. for you: calming down, apologizing, or using the tools? Why?

What are some kind things you could do for your Kindness Pal this week?

At Home:

If you find yourself in a conflict, practice using the Conflict C.A.T. this week.

Explain the C.A.T. to a friend of family member.

Unit 7
The Story I'm Telling Myself

Week 26
Remote Control Mindfulness

OBJECTIVES: Become aware of when minds wander

Practice noticing thoughts

Practice kindness

Prepare: A bell or chime

Your Kindness Pals list and Talking Object

Copies of the Remote Control worksheet for each student from the from the **Materials for Lessons Section**

This lesson helps the children notice their thoughts and make choices about which thoughts they want to focus on and which ones they'd like to let go.

You might like to reinforce the concept that having thoughts is normal, and that we are not asking them NOT to have thoughts. Instead, we are practicing the difficult skill of noticing our thoughts and then choosing to let them go if we want to.

When we recognize our thoughts, we have the opportunity to control our thoughts rather than allowing them to control us. This practice gives kids a way to notice what story they are telling themselves about future or past events, and to reflect on whether what they believe is actually true.

This lesson introduces the metaphor of a remote control and asks kids to consider who is pushing their buttons.

This would be a good time to remind students that participation in the mindfulness practice itself is always optional. Mindfulness is a practice that is meant to help them, and wholly for their own use and benefit. Remind students that if they ever feel uncomfortable or anxious during a practice, they may choose to do another practice such as Take 5 breathing or, with your permission, to mindfully walk across the back of the room, for example, as long as their choice does not disturb others.

Introduction

Ask: *What usually happens when I ask you to close your eyes and focus your mind on a sound or on your breath?*

Take a few answers.

Say: *Yes, one thing we all notice is that our minds wander. The good news is that this is perfectly normal. It happens to everyone.*

The difference is that when your mind wanders when you are in math class you might not notice it until the teacher calls on you and you suddenly realize you have no idea what is going on. That's not a great feeling.

In Mindfulness, we are trying to notice that moment when our minds wander and see where our minds go. Then we can decide if we want to redirect our minds. That's part of the fun.

It's sort of like you have a remote control in your mind. You might have decided to watch the "listen to the teacher channel" or the "do your math homework channel" but your mind might take the remote and change it to the "think about unicorns channel" or the "what's for dinner channel." This can happen when we are doing mindfulness too.

Today we are going to try to turn our remotes to the "Counting our Breaths Channel." Now this might not be the most exciting channel so we need to help it a bit. Try to get really curious about what breathing is like. What does it feel like? What is a whole breath? Where do you feel each part of your breath in your body? Do you feel it in your stomach, or chest or nose or throat? This curiosity might make it a little easier to keep your mind on this channel.

But our minds really like to change the channel, so as soon as you notice that instead of the "Counting Your Breaths" channel your mind has switched to the "I have a baseball game later" channel or the "Why did I say that embarrassing thing in music class yesterday?" channel, see if you can take the remote back and re-program it to the "Counting your Breaths" channel. You might have to change the channel over and over and that is perfectly fine. Trying to get better at this is one of the most useful things we can do!

Ready to try?

Mindfulness Practice: Remote Control Breathing

Invite today's Mindfulness Helper (MH) to come to the front of the class to sit next to you on a chair.

Prompt the MH to choose another student to turn off the classroom lights.

Prompt the MH to say: "Let's get into our mindful bodies. Close your eyes or look down into your lap. Let's take 3 deep breaths."

Say: *Now let your breath settle back into its natural rhythm. Just breathe. Put your hand on your belly to help you to focus on your breath.*

When you are ready, turn your remote control to the "Counting Your Breaths Channel" and start counting your breaths. Then just try to notice if you mind changes the channel and change it back. You might have to do this over and over. That's perfectly fine. Whenever you notice that your mind has changed the channel you might make a little gesture like you are changing the channel back.

Wait about a minute or so (or longer if it seems like they are able to do more) **and then say**: *Now you can just let your mind be free to think or not think.*

After a few moments, say: *Now let's take one more deep breath in and out. Let's listen to the sound mindfully and open your eyes or look up when you can't hear it anymore.*

Ask the MH to ring the bell

Ask the MH to choose a classmate to turn the lights on.

Ask the MH to return to his or her seat.

Reflect and Discuss

To prompt discussion, ask:

- Did your mind change the channel a lot or a little today?
- Was it tempting to stay on a different channel?
- Was it easy or hard to change the channel back?
- When could it be useful to redirect your focus?

Lesson: Remote Control Worksheet

Hand out copies of the Remote Control worksheet to all students.

Have students list any thoughts or feelings they remember having on the Remote Control Worksheet.

Share: Ask if anybody wants to share some of the channels they listed on their Worksheet.

Kindness Pals

Kindness Pal Activity: You can include some or all of the following as time allows, but do assign new Kindness Pals.

- Share kind acts from the previous week.
- Assign new Kindness Pals.
- Do the Kindness Pal Challenge (see Week 4).
- Share what you learned about your Kindness Pal with the group.

Closing words: *Okay our time is up for today. Thank you for a great class, everyone. Let's have a nice quiet moment for the bell. If you want to, you can close your eyes, picture your new Kindness Pal, and imagine yourself doing something kind for them this week.*

Ring the bell.

Extensions

Writing Prompts:

How could it be helpful to practice Remote Control breathing? Could it help you in school? Could it help you in your activities?

Can you think of a time when someone else "changed your channel"?

What are some kind things you could do for your Kindness Pal this week?

At Home:

Try noticing what channel your thoughts are on at home. Write down the thoughts and feelings you notice. Are they the same or different than the thoughts and feelings you noticed in class today?

Week 27
Where Are My Thoughts?

OBJECTIVES: Notice if thoughts are mostly about the past, present or future.

Practice kindness

Prepare: A bell or chime

Your Kindness Pals list and Talking Object

The object of this lesson is to help students keep their thoughts focused on the present. This helps students learn to direct their thoughts away from worries about the past or future, to notice when they are thinking about imaginary scenarios, and to stay in the present moment – helpful in school and in life!

Some of us are prone to worry and rumination. This practice offers a way to use mindful breathing to notice, allow and then manage this way of responding to challenging situations. This practice also gives students a way to manage their response to emotions inspired by others – to stay in control of their own responses.

Introduction

You might say:

The last time we met we practiced noticing our thoughts. We imagined that we had a remote control in our minds and noticed what channel we were on. Today we are going to try to notice if our thoughts are about the past, the present, or the future.

We might imagine that remote control again, but this time there are only three channels - you might think of them as The History Channel (the past), the Sci-Fi Channel (the future) and The Right Now Channel (the present). Do you remember doing this last year? It is actually a very challenging practice.

If I am thinking about my basketball game tomorrow my thoughts are in the... **(future)**. *The Sci-Fi Channel*

If I am thinking about an argument I had with my little brother last night, my thoughts are in the.... **(past)**. *The History Channel*

*If I am noticing that I am hungry my thoughts are in the…. (**present**). The Right Now Channel*

Sometimes you might notice that your thoughts aren't about the past, present or future but are just imaginings - maybe you are thinking about riding on a unicorn. That isn't something that you did in the past or will do in the future but just a different kind of thought.

What would be a good name for that channel? The Imagination Channel? The Anything Goes Channel? **Have them make their own names.**

Last time whenever we noticed that our minds had changed the channel we made a little changing channels gesture with our hands. Let's make up some new gestures for this game.

One way to do this is to say your left hand is for the past, your right hand is for the future and both hands in the middle is for the present. If you notice a past thought you could raise your left hand, if you notice a future thought you could raise your right hand, if you notice a present thought you can bring your hands together for a present thought.

Who can think of a gesture that would show that you were having an imaginary thought? **Take some ideas and let kids choose their own as long as they aren't distracting to others.**

Demonstrate this for your students *by narrating your own thoughts, labeling each one as in the past, present, future or imagination.*

If students ask questions about imaginary thoughts vs. future thoughts, you can let them know it doesn't really matter what they call the thoughts, but it is important to notice them and to try to let them go to come back to the present moment.

Say*: So today, after we get set up by the Mindfulness Helper, we are going to try to count our breaths.*

Only this time, every time you notice that your mind has wandered (and you know it will!) I want you to try to notice if it is a thought about the past, the present, the future, or an imaginary thought. You'll do your hand gesture and then try to start again focusing on your breath.

Once you've labeled that thought, see if you can bring your mind back to counting your breaths.

Before we start, make sure that you have decided what your hand gestures are going to be for past, present, future, and imagination.

Mindfulness Practice: Past-Present-Future

Invite today's Mindfulness Helper (MH) to come to the front of the class and sit next to you on a chair.

Prompt the MH to choose another student to turn off the classroom lights.

Prompt the MH to say: "Let's get into our mindful bodies. Close your eyes or look down into your lap. Let's take 3 deep breaths.

You might say: Now try to count your breaths or keep your mind focused on your breath in whichever way you like.

When you notice that your focus has wandered away from your breathing, notice if you are thinking about something that happened in the past or the future, or whether it is about something that is happening right now. Do your hand gesture and start again. Remember it is totally normal to have to start over and over.

After a few moments, say: Now let's take one more deep breath in and out. Let's listen to the sound mindfully and open your eyes or look up when you can't hear it anymore.

Ask the MH to ring the bell.

Ask the MH to choose a classmate to turn the lights on.

Ask the MH to return to his or her seat.

Reflect and Discuss

After the exercise is over say:

- Raise your hand if most of your thoughts were about the past.
- Raise your hand if most of your thoughts were in the present.
- Raise your hand if most of your thoughts were in the future.
- Raise your hand if most of your thoughts were imaginary.
- Raise your hand if you had a mixture.

Ask some of the children to share one of the thoughts they noticed and then **let other children guess** if the thought was in the past, present, or future.

This isn't always easy and there can be more than one right answer.

Ask:

- Why do you think it might be good to keep your mind focused on the present, on this moment?
- If your mind is always focused on what has already happened, or what hasn't happened yet, or what might never happen, what do you think you might be missing?

Point Out:

- When we try to notice where our thoughts are going, we can try to redirect them to where we want them to be. If you tend to worry a lot, your thoughts are mostly in the…. (future).
- Worrying doesn't help make things better and it doesn't stop bad things from happening. But it does keep you from enjoying the good stuff.
- If you notice that your thoughts are often in the future, see if you can try to focus your mind on something right here in the present moment. Try to notice what is good in this moment.
- Perhaps share an example from your own life of the value of focusing on the present moment, instead of on the past or future.

Optional Activity: Repeat the Worksheet lesson from the previous week but use the names of the Past, Present, Future Channels.

Kindness Pals

Kindness Pal Activity: You can include some or all of the following as time allows, but do assign new Kindness Pals.

- Share kind acts from the previous week.
- Assign new Kindness Pals.
- Do the Kindness Pal Challenge (see Week 4).
- Share what you learned about your Kindness Pal with the group.

Closing words: *Okay our time is up for today. Thank you for a great class everyone. Let's have a nice quiet moment for the bell. If you want to, you can close your eyes, picture your new Kindness Pal, and imagine yourself doing something kind for them this week.*

Ring the bell.

Extensions

Writing Prompts:

How could it be helpful to practice past-present-future breathing? Could it help you in school? Could it help you in your activities?

What are some kind things you could do for your Kindness Pal this week?

At Home:

Try noticing where your thoughts are a few times this week. Are they mostly in the past, the present or the future? When you feel worried, where are your thoughts? When you feel really happy, where are your thoughts?

Week 28:
Fast and Slow Thinking

OBJECTIVES: Learn about Fast and Slow Thinking and relate the concept to earlier lessons

Explore how Fast and Slow Thinking can be both helpful and challenging

Practice kindness

PREPARE: A bell or chime

6 Copies of the Skit: *The Story I'm Telling Myself* found in the **Materials for Lessons** Section.

Your Kindness Pals list and Talking Object

In this lesson, we introduce the concept of Fast and Slow Thinking that Nobel Laureate Daniel Kahneman explores in his book *Thinking, Fast and Slow*. This approach gives students another way to understand the role of the amygdala and the PFC and the brain's negativity bias. It also emphasizes the value of the mindfulness practice of noticing our thoughts, and taking time to consider whether what we are thinking is really true.

Introduction

You might say: *One benefit of learning to notice and pay attention to our thoughts is that this practice gives us an opportunity to notice what the story is that we're telling ourselves about a situation, and to ask if the story is really true. Is what I'm assuming really true? Is it false? Or do I just not know?*

Today we are going to learn about the ways our brain thinks fast, and thinks slow. It's really amazing how our brain works - we'll get a little more insight. When it comes to how we treat other people sometimes our fast thinking can get us into trouble - we'll explore that too.

But first, our mindfulness practice.

Mindfulness Practice

Invite today's Mindfulness Helper (MH) to come to the front of the class and sit next to you on a chair.

Prompt the MH to choose another student to turn off the classroom lights.

Prompt the MH to say: "Let's get into our mindful bodies. Close your eyes or look down into your lap. Let's take 3 deep breaths."

Say: *When you notice that your focus has wandered away from your breathing, notice if you are thinking about something that happened in the past or the future, or whether it is about something that is happening right now.*

Bring your mind back to your breathing. You might want to try counting your breaths to help you, or doing the balancing breath we learned a couple of weeks ago.

After a few moments, say: *Now let's take one more deep breath in and out. Let's listen to the sound mindfully and open your eyes or look up when you can't hear it anymore.*

Ask the MH to ring the bell.

Ask the MH to choose a classmate to turn the lights on.

Ask the MH to return to his or her seat.

Lesson: Fast and Slow Thinking

1. **System 1, System 2 and Bias**

    Say: *Today we are going to be learning something new about our brains. Researchers have discovered that our brains have two ways of thinking - fast and slow - also known as System 1 (fast) and System 2 (slow).*

    Our fast brain (System 1) is our "gut reaction" when we react without thinking. Does this sound familiar? We learned about a part of our brain that operates without thinking - The amygdala. The amygdala is like our threat detection center and is incredibly important for keeping us safe.

    Our slow brain (System 2) is the way of thinking that reflects on things, takes in the information, and makes decisions. This sounds a bit like what the PFC does.

    Ask: *Can you think of an example of fast thinking that would be helpful?*

    Offer an example: *You see a ball coming toward you and you cover your face or quickly try to catch it.*

    Ask: *Would slow thinking be helpful in that scenario?*

    Answer: *No, you don't want to think too hard about a ball that is coming at you. You want to react quickly.*

    Ask: *Can you think of an example of fast thinking that would be unhelpful?*

Take some answers and offer an example:

> Maybe there is a new kid in your class and he is wearing a Yankees baseball jersey. You are a Boston Red Sox fan and those two teams have a longstanding rivalry. What might your fast thinking brain decide about that kid?
>
> That he loves the Yankees, therefore he hates the Red Sox, therefore he is not on your side, therefore you don't want to be friends with him.
>
> What would your slow thinking brain decide: Hey that kid is wearing a Yankees jersey. I wonder if he likes baseball as much as I do? Maybe I'll go ask him if he likes to play baseball…
>
> Then maybe when you ask him he says that it is his brother's jersey and he doesn't really like the Yankees - that he's more into soccer.

Say: *That is an example of how when we go only by fast thinking we might get things totally wrong about people and situations.*

We're lucky that our brains have the capacity to do fast and slow thinking. When it comes to how we treat other people sometimes our fast thinking, System 1 thinking can become a problem.

Do you remember when we learned about the Negativity Bias? How it can be really helpful in keeping us safe but can also cause us to forget about and not notice so many good things in our lives? Well fast thinking can also cause us sometimes to make snap judgments about people that can be wrong and harmful.

2. **Skit:** *The Story I'm Telling Myself*

   Introduce the skit: *Today we are going to be acting out a skit about how fast thinking can lead us to make up stories that aren't really true. This is something that almost everybody does but once we start to notice it we can try to decide if that story is helpful to us or not.*

   Choose 6 actors to play Julio, Hassan, Tianna, Mom, Narrator 1 and Narrator 2.

   Hand out copies of the skit and have them act it out.

   Have the audience notice examples of fast and slow thinking in the skit.

Reflect and Discuss

1. Was Hassan doing fast or slow thinking when he heard his friends talking about his song?

2. Why didn't he challenge his fast thinking when he was talking to his mom about it?

3. What would you have done if you thought that you heard your friends saying something mean about you?

4. How could mindfulness help you to take a moment to do some slow thinking?

Kindness Pals

Kindness Pal Activity: You can include some or all of the following as time allows, but do assign new Kindness Pals.

- Share kind acts from the previous week.
- Assign new Kindness Pals.
- Do the Kindness Pal Challenge (see Week 4).
- Share what you learned about your Kindness Pal with the group.

Closing words: *Okay our time is up for today. Thank you for a great class, everyone. Let's have a nice quiet moment for the bell. If you want to, you can close your eyes, picture your new Kindness Pal, and imagine yourself doing something kind for them this week.*

Ring the bell.

Extensions

Writing Prompts:

Write about some examples of fast and slow thinking in your own life.

What are some kind things you could do for your Kindness Pal this week?

At Home:

Notice a time when you were thinking fast. Was fast thinking helpful or not in that case?

Notice a time when you were thinking slow. Was slow thinking helpful or not in that case?

Week 29
Don't Believe Everything You Think

OBJECTIVES: Learn about and discuss implicit bias and stereotypes

Practice kindness

PREPARE: A bell or chime

Your Kindness Pals list and Talking Object

Means to show a video: *Run Like a Girl* https://youtu.be/XjJQBjWYDTs

This lesson introduces the challenging topics of stereotypes and bias. The goal here is to introduce a discussion, and to invite kids to consider that: we all have biases - that's normal - but when it comes to how we think about other people, it is important to try to notice our biases and then decide whether we want to change them. We'll look together at some common stereotypes and watch a discussion-provoking video called "Run like a Girl." You might like to watch this before class and notice where the timing cues are. **Be sure to have the video set up in advance in order to avoid the commercials that may not be appropriate**.

One note on the video: "Run Like a Girl" is made by a company that sells products to girls and women. We are in no way endorsing the product or the company, nor do we have any relationship with the company of any kind.

Mindfulness can help us approach these topics with compassion for ourselves and others. Mindfulness helps us to notice that our thoughts and biases are just thoughts, not facts. If we can notice that we have them then we can take some time to decide if we actually believe them or not.

Introduction

You might say: Today we are going to be noticing our thoughts and learning about how our thoughts can affect the way we think about and treat others. We'll be thinking about fast and slow thinking and applying what we've learned in a discussion about gender stereotypes.

As always, let's start with our Mindfulness Practice. Today we are going to do the Remote Control Breathing Practice.

Mindfulness Practice

Invite today's Mindfulness Helper (MH) to come to the front of the class and sit next to you on a chair.

Prompt the MH to choose another student to turn off the classroom lights.

Prompt the MH to say: "Let's get into our mindful bodies. Close your eyes or look down into your lap. Let's take 3 deep breaths."

Say: *Now let your breath settle back into its natural rhythm. Just breathe. Put your hand on your belly to help you to focus on your breath.*

When you are ready, turn your remote control to the "Counting Your Breaths Channel" and start counting your breaths. Then just try to notice if you mind changes the channel and change it back. You might have to do this over and over. That's perfectly fine. Whenever you notice that your mind has changed the channel you might make a little gesture like you are changing the channel back.

Wait about a minute or so (or longer if it seems like they are able to do more) **and then say**: *Now you can just let your mind be free to think or not think.*

After a few moments, say: *Now let's take one more deep breath in and out. Let's listen to the sound mindfully and open your eyes or look up when you can't hear it anymore.*

Ask the MH to ring the bell when the Remote Control breathing exercise is complete.

Ask the MH to choose a classmate to turn the lights on.

Ask the MH to return to his or her seat.

Lesson: Stereotypes and Bias

1. **Addressing bias and stereotypes**

    You might introduce this lesson by saying: *Do you remember the Weird-Dare-Tough stories we discussed earlier in the year? Bullying is one kind of unkindness.*

    Sometimes people are bullied or mistreated because they are perceived as "different."

Sometimes we perceive people as different and have negative feelings about them without even realizing it. This is called implicit or unconscious bias. Everybody has this kind of bias. Having biases doesn't make you a bad person - it's part of being human.

Sometimes our biases can be a way of protecting us. Do you remember learning about the Negativity Bias in Week 14? The Negativity Bias is something that our brains do to help to keep us safe. If we burn our hand on a hot stove or a coffee pot our brain will remember that so that we don't do it again. That is a helpful and important bias.

But when it comes to how we think about other people it is important to try to notice our biases and then decide whether we want to change them. Mindfulness can help because mindfulness helps us to notice that our thoughts and biases are just thoughts, not facts. If we can notice that we have them then we can take some time to decide if we actually believe them or not.

> *"Not everything that is faced can be changed, but nothing can be changed until it is faced."*
> *— James Baldwin*

For the next few lessons we are going to be focusing on gender bias and gender stereotypes.

2. **Stereotypes: True? Fair? Hurtful?**

   For example - a stereotype that some people believe is that girls aren't as athletic as boys.

   Ask:

   - Is this always true?
   - Is this an unfair belief?
   - Could this thought be hurtful to girls?
   - Is this a bias?

   Take a few answers.

   Say: *So it's a bias we need to look at. We can study this in ourselves, and think about what we can do to change our reactions. Mindfulness can help.*

   Ask: *Can you think of some other examples of these kinds of biases?*

   Take a few answers.

Point out: *Biases are sometimes based on stereotypes. A stereotype is an often unfair and untrue belief that many people have about all people or things with a particular characteristic - like gender or skin color or ability.*

Ask: Can you *think* of an example of a stereotype about tall people?

Take a few answers.

Say: *Yes, some people assume tall people are good at basketball.*

Ask: Do some tall people like basketball? Are some tall people good at basketball? Does that mean that all tall people are good at basketball? No

Ask: *Can you think of a stereotype about people who wear glasses?*

Take a few answers.

Say: *Yes, some people assume people who wear glasses are smart or nerdy.*

Ask: *Are all people who wear glasses smart? Nerdy?* No.

Ask: *Are these stereotypes hurtful? Sometimes. Are they a serious problem or dangerous? Sometimes.*

Ask: *What would make a stereotype a serious problem or dangerous?*

Take a few answers.

You might say: *One answer is Power. If a group of people has more power in our society, then stereotypes the powerful group may have about the group that has less power may be used to harm them, (either on purpose or without realizing it).*

Ask: *Have you ever felt like someone was treated you badly because of a stereotype about someone who looks like you?*

Take some answers.

3. **Revisit the THiNK Test**

   Remind your students about the THiNK Test that we learned in Weeks 9 and 10.

   Say: *Let's see if some of these stereotypes pass the THiNK Test…*

   Say these out loud and ask students to share their thoughts.

   > **"Tall people are good at basketball."**
   > - Is it True?

- Is it Helpful?
- Is it Necessary?
- Is it Kind?

Ask: *What do you think? Does it pass the THiNK Test? Let's try another:*

"Girls aren't good at sports."

- Is it True?
- Is it Helpful?
- Is it Necessary?
- Is it Kind?

Ask: *What do you think? Can the THiNK Test be a good way of helping us to think about stereotypes and bias?*

Offer some context: *Over the next few lessons we are going to be thinking more about stereotypes and bias based on gender. In the past it was very obvious that women had less power in society than men. Women weren't granted the right to vote until more than 100 years after men. In the past women were barred from many careers and schools and were unable to own their own property. Times have changed dramatically but many stereotypes about women still exist. Some are so common that we don't even notice them.*

4. **Watch video: "Run Like a Girl"**

Say: *Let's watch this video about the stereotypes many of us still have - in this case, about what it means to do something "like a girl."*

Watch the video: https://youtu.be/XjJQBjWYDTs

Stop the video at 00:39

Reflect and Discuss

Use these questions to guide a discussion:

- What do you think about this?
- Did you notice that everybody did basically the same thing when they were asked to run or throw or fight like a girl?
- Where do you think these ideas or stereotypes come from?

Resume the video and stop it again at 1:09

Use these questions to guide a discussion:

- Why do you think the little girls had a different response to the question "What does it mean to run like a girl?"
- How does it make you feel to see the answers of the little girls?
- Where do you think the idea of doing something "like a girl" came from?
- Why is it still a common bias even though we have lots of examples of amazing women athletes like Serena Williams and Megan Rapinoe?
- Do you think that the people who were asked to "run like a girl" thought that they were biased against girls?
- What would it sound like to you if I said that somebody "did math like a girl" or "wrote an essay like a girl"?
- How do you think taking time to think about and notice our thoughts could be helpful?

Say: *Implicit or unconscious bias is an attitude, judgment or stereotype that we have without even realizing it. All people have some kind of implicit bias against others. We can't change those biases until we recognize that we have them.*

In the next few lessons we are going to learn a little more about implicit bias and how we can use what we have learned about mindfulness, brain science, and kindness to think about how we treat other people.

Kindness Pals

Kindness Pal Activity: You can include some or all of the following as time allows, but do assign new Kindness Pals.

- Share kind acts from the previous week.
- Assign new Kindness Pals.
- Do the Kindness Pal Challenge (see Week 4).
- Share what you learned about your Kindness Pal with the group.

Closing words: *Okay our time is up for today. Thank you for a great class, everyone. Let's have a nice quiet moment for the bell. If you want to, you can close your eyes, picture your new Kindness Pal, and imagine yourself doing something kind for them this week.*

Ring the bell.

Extensions

Writing Prompts:

Can you think of other examples of stereotypes?

Have you ever felt like you were being treated differently because of stereotypes about people who look like you?

What are some kind things you could do for your Kindness Pal this week?

At Home:

Notice when you might be assuming something about someone because of a stereotype that might not be true.

Week 30
Gender Stereotyping

OBJECTIVES: Learn about and discuss gender stereotypes

Practice kindness

PREPARE: A bell or chime

9 Copies of Skit: *Who's Moving In*? found in the **Materials for Lessons** Section.

Copies of Gender Stereotype Worksheet for each student found in the **Materials for Lessons** Section

Your Kindness Pals list and Talking Object

In this lesson we are going to be thinking more about gender stereotypes. We'll do a skit to help us to notice how these stereotypes are part of our everyday beliefs and how they affect how we think about and treat others.

Introduction

Say: *Today we are going to be thinking more about gender stereotypes. We'll act out a skit and work with our Kindness Pals to help us to notice stereotypes about boys and girls that we might not even know that we have.*

Mindfulness practice is really helpful in this work, so let's start with that.

Mindfulness Practice

Invite today's Mindfulness Helper (MH) to come to the front of the class to sit next to you on a chair.

Prompt the MH to choose another student to turn off the classroom lights.

Prompt the MH to say: "Let's get into our mindful bodies. Close your eyes or look down into your lap. Let's take 3 deep breaths."

Say: *Now let your breath settle back into its natural rhythm. Just breathe. Put your hand on your belly to help you to focus on your breath.*

When you are ready, turn your remote control to the "Counting Your Breaths Channel" and start counting your breaths. Then just try to notice if you mind

changes the channel and change it back. You might have to do this over and over. That's perfectly fine. Whenever you notice that your mind has changed the channel you might make a little gesture like you are changing the channel back.

Wait about a minute or so (or longer if it seems like they are able to do more) **and then say**: *Now you can just let your mind be free to think or not think.*

After a few moments, say: *Now let's take one more deep breath in and out. Let's listen to the sound mindfully and open your eyes or look up when you can't hear it anymore.*

Ask the MH to ring the bell

Ask the MH to choose a classmate to turn the lights on.

Ask the MH to return to his or her seat.

Lesson: Who's Moving In?

Introduce the skit: *To explore the idea of gender bias, we'll act out a skit called "Who's moving in?" In this skit, four kids are trying to guess the gender of a child named Indigo moving into their apartment based on their belongings.*

> *NOTE: You can cast "Indigo" with either a boy or a girl. Indigo's gender is not revealed in the skit - it is left to the students to make their own guess.*

Invite volunteers to act out 9 parts.

Hand out skits and have your students act it out.

Reflect and Discuss

Use these questions to guide a discussion:

1. Do you think Indigo is a girl or a boy?
2. Why did Teddy and Keiko think that they could tell by Indigo's stuff if they were a girl or a boy?
3. Would you have agreed with some of these guesses? Why?
4. What would you have thought if the parents had carried in a baby doll?
5. Were the kids' ideas about Indigo formed by gender stereotypes?

6. What gender stereotypes did you hear in this skit?

7. Does it matter if Indigo is a girl or a boy?

Activity: Talking about Gender Stereotypes

Assign New Kindness Pals

Hand out Gender Stereotypes Worksheet

Instruct: *Now you are going to be working with your Kindness Pal to think about some different objects. You'll think about whether you associate that object with boys or girls. Make sure to talk about why you have that association.*

It's okay if you disagree! You can write down both of your answers. If you are not sure, try using the THiNK Test like we did last week and see if that helps.

Have kids share their answers.

Say: *Next time we are going to talk about what we can do when we hear people saying things that you think are based on stereotypes and are examples of implicit bias.*

Kindness Pals

Kindness Pal Activity: You can include some or all of the following as time allows.

- Share kind acts from the previous week.
- Do the Kindness Pal Challenge (see Week 4).
- Share what you learned about your Kindness Pal with the group.

Closing words: *Okay our time is up for today. Thank you for a great class, everyone. Let's have a nice quiet moment for the bell. If you want to, you can close your eyes, picture your new Kindness Pal, and imagine yourself doing something kind for them this week.*

Ring the bell.

Extensions

Writing Prompts:

Did you learn something about your own beliefs that surprised you today?

What are some kind things you could do for your Kindness Pal this week?

At Home:

Have kids look through toy catalogs, magazines, or do an internet search to look for examples of gender stereotyping in advertising.

Week 31
Using Mindfulness to Interrupt Bias

OBJECTIVES: Help to build the courage, confidence and skills to stand up for ourselves and others.

Practice kindness

PREPARE: A real bell or chime

6 copies of the skit *Dude!* found in the **Materials for Lessons** Section

Your Kindness Pals list

Sometimes when kids are angry, or upset by bullying or unkindness, they don't know what to say or can't think of anything in the moment. That's why something simple like the word "Dude" can help.

In this week's skit, we use the word "Dude" to show that one word can be powerful enough to change the course of another person's actions.

If "Dude" isn't the word that your kids would use to show their disapproval of another kid's actions, feel free to substitute a word that is more meaningful to your students.

Introduction

Say: Today we're going to act out a skit and learn something that you can try if you want to speak up when you hear someone say something mean or biased.

But first, let's do our mindfulness practice. Today we're going to do our Heartfulness practice again. We've been talking about a lot of hard things in the last few classes. You might have noticed that you have some biases and you might feel bad about some things that you have said in the past. It's really important to remember that these biases are not our fault. We have learned them from advertising or from adults who might not even realize that they have them.

It's important to be kind and patient with ourselves and others as we learn and grow. Making the world a more peaceful place is hard work! Let's try to do it with kindness.

Mindfulness Practice

Consult your alphabetical roll list, and choose the next student to be the Mindfulness Helper for the day.

Invite the Mindfulness Helper (MH) to come to the front of the class to sit next to you on a chair.

Prompt the MH to choose another student to turn off the classroom lights.

Prompt the MH to say: "Let's get into our mindful bodies. Close your eyes or look down into your lap. Let's take 3 deep breaths."

Say: *Today we are going to do our Heartfulness practice again. This is when we think kind thoughts about people in our mind. Today let's think about someone you have helped, someone who has helped you, and ourselves.*

Say: *Take a deep breath.*

First, Let's think about someone you have helped.

If you'd like to, put your hand over your heart and repeat these words in your mind while you think about this person:

May you be happy. **Wait a moment.**

May you be healthy. **Wait a moment.**

May you be peaceful. **Wait a moment**.

Take a moment to notice how you feel. Any way that you feel is fine, even if you feel nothing. Just try to notice it.

Next, Let's think about someone who has helped you.

If you'd like to, put your hand over your heart and repeat these words in your mind while you think about this person:

May you be happy. **Wait a moment.**

May you be healthy. **Wait a moment.**

May you be peaceful. **Wait a moment.**

Take a moment to notice how you feel. Any way that you feel is fine, even if you feel nothing. Just try to notice it.

Finally, let's think about ourselves.

If you'd like to, put your hand over your heart and repeat these words in your mind while you think about yourself:

May I be happy. **Wait a moment.**

May I be healthy. **Wait a moment.**

May I be peaceful. **Wait a moment**.

Take a moment to notice how you feel. Any way that you feel is fine, even if you feel nothing. Just try to notice it.

Cue the MH to ring the bell when the Heartfulness practice is complete.

Cue the MH to choose a classmate to turn the lights on.

Ask the MH to return to his or her seat.

After a few moments, say: *Now let's take one more deep breath in and out. Let's listen to the sound mindfully and open your eyes or look up when you can't hear it anymore.*

Ask the MH to ring the bell when the mindful breathing is complete.

Ask the MH to choose a classmate to turn the lights on.

Ask the MH to return to his or her seat.

Lesson: Responding to unfair or unkind treatment of another

1. **What to say?**

    Say: *In the past few lessons we've been learning about stereotypes and implicit or unconscious bias. Now that we are starting to become more aware of our own biases, we might also start to notice them in others.*

    Often when we hear someone say something mean to someone - whether it is bullying or whether it is a mean comment based on a stereotype or bias - we might really want to speak up and say something.

    It's important to remember that in real life we don't have someone writing our words for us. And it can be hard to think of something to say in the moment, especially when you are upset by what is happening.

    Our mindfulness practice can help us to take a moment and breathe before we speak so that we can really think about what we want to say.

    Speaking up is important. Every time we call out bias or stereotypes we change the way people think and help people to notice their thoughts. It doesn't change overnight but little by little we can change the world.

2. **Skit: *Dude!***

   Introduce the Skit: *In this skit called "Dude" there are 6 kids on the playground: Richard, Benson, Aniyah, Andrew, Kidus, and Emmanuel. We need 6 volunteers to act out this skit. If we have time, we may be able to do it again with 6 more.*

   The audience has an important role here. As you hear the characters talk to each other, notice how your body feels. Notice if you have felt any of these feelings before in a similar situation. Notice if you hear examples of implicit or unconscious bias.

   Assign roles and have students act out the skit.

Reflect and Discuss

You might use these questions to shape a discussion:

- What do you think of the way the kids handled this situation?
- Did you notice any feelings in your body during the skit?
- Did you think the word "Dude" was helpful here? Why?
- Is there another word or phrase that you might use instead?
- Have you ever wanted to stand up for someone but couldn't think of what to say? It can be hard to think of the right thing. Do you think saying something like "Dude" would be easier?
- Have you seen bullying, teasing, or examples of this kind of bias in tv, movies or books? How have you noticed kids handling it? What have you noticed that works and doesn't work?

If you have time, allow another 6 students to act out the skit.

Say: *Standing up for people and standing up against bias is hard. It takes courage and the ability to remain calm so that you can really say what you want to say. We hope that in Peace Class you have learned a set of tools that will help you feel more equipped to stand up for yourself and others. The more we call out bias and stereotypes the sooner we will get rid of them. And that will be better for all of us.*

Kindness Pals

Kindness Pal Activity: You can include some or all of the following as time allows, but do assign new Kindness Pals.

- Share kind acts from the previous week.

- Assign new Kindness Pals.
- Do the Kindness Pal Challenge.
- Share what you learned about your Kindness Pal with the group.

Closing words: *Okay our time is up for today. Thank you for a great class, everyone. Let's have a nice quiet moment for the bell. If you want to, you can close your eyes, picture your new Kindness Pal, and imagine yourself doing something kind for them this week.*

Ring the bell.

Extensions

Writing Prompts:

Could you imagine yourself using "Dude" in this way? Another word?

Have you ever wanted to speak up but didn't say anything because you didn't know what to say?

What are some kind things you could do for your Kindness Pal this week?

At Home:

Encourage children to notice situations in which they could stand up for someone else, and try using a "one word" approach.

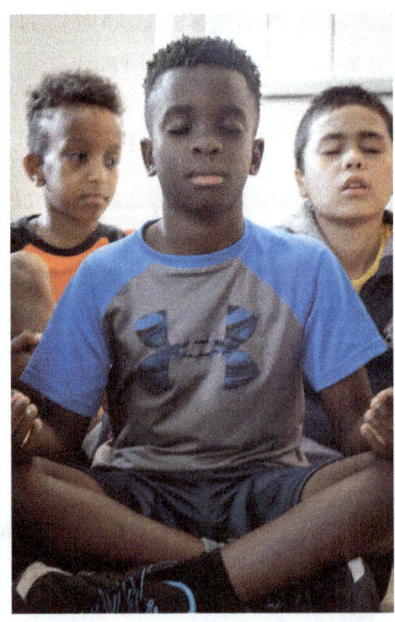

Unit 8
Closing out the Year

Week 32
Kindest Things

OBJECTIVES: Encourage the children to see the good in each other and experience the good feeling of sharing heartfelt compliments

PREPARE: Paper, pen or pencil for every student in the class

> NOTE FROM LINDA: This is a wonderful activity that has been very meaningful to my students over the years. It is a bit time-consuming for the teacher because you are going to be typing up a page for each child that lists all of the kind things the class said about him or her. I hope that you will do it anyway.
>
> I have found that I learn more about my students from what they say about other people than from what others say about them. I have had many students tell me that they have kept their Kindest Things page on their walls all the way through college! It's worth the work. I've done it for up to 100 kids every year and it is time well-spent.

Mindfulness Practice

Invite today's Mindfulness Helper (MH) to come to the front of the class to sit next to you on a chair.

Prompt the MH to choose another student to turn off the classroom lights.

Prompt the MH to say: "Let's get into our mindful bodies. Close your eyes or look down into your lap. Let's take 3 deep breaths."

Check to see that all students are sitting comfortably with their eyes closed or looking down.

Say: I'd like you to think about someone who makes you happy. Choose someone you see every day at home or at school. You might choose someone in your family, a friend, teacher, even a pet. Just choose someone and try to picture that person happy and smiling. Picture them doing something that *makes them happy. Try to notice how you feel when you think about this person.*

Now, if you'd like to, fill your heart up with kindness and repeat these words in your mind while you think about this person:

May you be happy. **Wait a moment.**

May you be healthy. **Wait a moment.**

May you be peaceful. **Wait a moment.**

Take a moment to notice how you feel. Any way that you feel is fine, even if you feel nothing. Just try to notice it.

Invite the students to share whom they were thinking about.

After a few moments, say: *Now let's take one more deep breath in and out. Let's listen to the sound mindfully and open your eyes or look up when you can't hear it anymore.*

Ask the MH to ring the bell when the mindful breathing is complete.

Ask the MH to choose a classmate to turn the lights back on.

Ask the MH to return to his or her seat.

Lesson: Kindest Things

1. **Setting the tone**

   Read these instructions aloud.

   These instructions are long, but it's really important that the kids get the sense of reverence in this activity.

   Say: *Today we are going to do something very powerful. We have talked about how we can use our words to hurt or to help others. Today we are going to use our words to be kind to each other.*

   I am going to ask you to think about the kindest thing you can think of to say about each person in the class.

   We are going to go one by one. I will say the name of someone in the class and write that person's name on the board. You will write down one or two things about that person.

   You might think about what is special about that person—a talent they have, a time when they were kind to you, maybe they are always friendly to new *people, maybe they always make you laugh, maybe you admire them for being brave, or creative or artistic, etc. Do **not** just use the first thing that pops into your head.*

You will write your name on your paper, but only I will see it. Each comment will be anonymous.

IMPORTANT: There will be absolutely no talking during this exercise. We are holding each person in the class in our kindness circle. Giggling or talking can sometimes lead to accidental unkindness or misunderstandings. Anyone who cannot abide by the rule of silence will be asked to wait in the hall and will not participate.

After class, I will type up a paper for each one of you with all of the kind things your classmates said about you. You won't be able to see who said what, but you will see what they said. This will take me a while, but I will return them to you soon. Make sure that you share the paper I give you with your family!

2. **Kindest Things exercise**

    Lead the class through the exercise.

    Write the first student's name on the board so everyone can see the spelling.

    Say: *"Now we will think about (Name). What is the kindest thing you can think of to say about (Name)? What is special about (Name)?"*

    Give a minute or more for students to write kind things about each child depending on how much time you have. If necessary, remind the class that this is a silent activity.

    When the exercise is over, give them time to catch up on anybody they missed and then collect the papers.

    Ask the class to share what this experience was like for them.

Kindness Pals

Kindness Pal Activity: Share kind acts from the previous week.

Do not give out new Kindness Pals, as this is the last week before the Capstone Project.

Closing words: *Okay our time is up for today. Thank you for a great class, everyone. Let's have a nice quiet moment for the bell. If you want to, you can close your eyes, picture your new Kindness Pal, and imagine yourself doing something kind for them this week.*

Ring the bell.

Week 33
Capstone Project

OBJECTIVES: Support students in summing up what they have learned this year. Have students consider how they will put their new skills to work.

PREPARE: Pen or pencil for every student in the class.

A piece of paper or poster board for each student in the class (8x11 or larger)

Markers, collage materials

A list of topics covered since Week 1 on the board. See the At-a-Glance in Section III for a recap of mindfulness practices and lesson objectives for the year.

In this final class, the students will make a representation of what they are going to take away from this year's **Peace of Mind** class. This isn't an assessment, but rather a chance for your students to reflect back on the year and think about how they can go forward and incorporate what they have learned in their lives.

Please feel free to put your own creative spin on this project, and make any modifications you need to in order to meet the needs of your class.

Introduction

Say: *Today is our final Peace Class of this year. We are going to take some time to reflect on what we have learned together this year. Then we are going to be making something that will help us to remember some of the many things we have learned and make some plans for how we will put our new skills to work.*

First, let's do our mindfulness practice together for the last time this year.

Mindfulness Practice

Your choice: either follow the familiar framework below, or you might consider letting your students do their own practice unguided.

Invite the final Mindfulness Helper (MH) of the year to come to the front of the class and sit next to you on a chair.

Prompt the MH to choose another student to turn off the classroom lights.

Prompt the MH to say: "Let's get into our mindful bodies. Close your eyes or look down into your lap. Let's take 3 deep breaths."

Say: *Choose your own practice.*

After a few moments, say: *Now let's take one more deep breath in and out. Let's listen to the sound mindfully and open your eyes or look up when you can't hear it anymore.*

Ask the MH to ring the bell when the exercise is complete.

Ask the MH to choose a classmate to turn the lights on**.**

Ask the MH to return to his or her seat.

Lesson: Creative Summing Up

Review The Year

Refer to the list you put on the board of what you have covered this year.

Reflect on how much you have explored together.

Have the kids briefly share what they remember about each section.

Say: *Now we are going to make something that will help us to sum up what we've been doing this year. You can make a poster, a poem, a collage, an essay, a drawing, anything you want. There are a few things that I want you to include in your project:*

- At least five things that you remember learning in Peace of Mind class
- At least two ways of doing mindfulness
- At least two ways that you will use something you learned in Peace of Mind Class in your real life
- At least one way that you think you can make the world a better place because of something you learned in Peace of Mind Class.
- Got it? Okay, let's be creative!

Have the students share their creations when they are finished. We hope these will be reminders for them of all that they have learned this year, and how they can put their skills to work.

Closing words: *I hope that you enjoyed learning more about mindfulness, and kindness, and how to work out our conflicts peacefully. The world needs lots of kind, mindful people. Now you have some tools to help you go out into the world and make it a more peaceful place. I hope you will!*

VI. Materials for Lessons

Skits

All of the skits included in this curriculum are original works by Linda Ryden, written specifically for the *Peace of Mind* curriculum.

Week 19	Elijah's Brain	Brain science
Week 20	Swings are for Babies	Conflict resolution
Week 28	The Story I'm Telling Myself	Fast and slow Thinking
Week 30	Who is Moving In?	Gender Stereotypes
Week 31	"Dude"	Standing up against bullying

Week 19 Skit
Elijah's Brain

Topic:	Brain Science
4 Characters:	Elijah, PFC, Amygdala, Hippocampus (Hippo)
Prepare:	Make signs for the brain parts
Setting:	School basketball game. Elijah is preparing to shoot a free throw. His amygdala, PFC and hippocampus are shouting at him from the stands.

PFC: Okay Elijah, you got this. Stay calm and focus on making the shot.

Hippo: Remember what the coach said, aim for the backboard.

Amygdala: Oh no, what if he misses? He's starting to sweat!

PFC: No, it's okay Elijah, just breathe and focus.

Hippo: Remember to bend your knees when you shoot.

Amygdala: No, this is terrible! He's going to miss and then everybody is going to be disappointed and we're going to lose the game!

And hey isn't that Manuel? He's going to make fun of you if you miss.

I'm freaking out!

PFC: Wait, Elijah…

Amygdala: That's enough PFC - I'm going to turn you off!

PFC: Noooooo!!!

Hippo: But Elijah, don't forget…

Amygdala: You too, Hippocampus, off you go. I have a plan. He's going to stand here frozen and then if that doesn't work he can throw the ball really hard and run out of the gym. Perfect!

Hippo: That's terrible advice! Amygdala is just trying to help you but you need to think.

PFC: Do your Take Five breathing!

Elijah starts to do Take Five breathing, tracing one hand with a finger of the other hand, breathing in as he goes up, and out as he goes down.

Amygdala: Wait, what's he doing? Deep breathing? But that means I don't have to be in charge anymore….

PFC: All right! Okay Elijah you got this. Focus!

Hippo: Don't forget to bend your knees Elijah!!

Elijah makes the shot. Everybody cheers!

The End

Week 20 Skit
Swings are for Babies

Topic: Going up and down the Conflict Escalator
Characters: Dakota, Derrick, Dawson, Mateo, Tamera
Setting: Playground

Dakota: Hey guys, let's go on the swings!

Derrick: No, I want to play basketball.

Dawson: Me too. The swings are for babies.

Zion: What?! The swings are fun!

Tamera: You're being mean, Dawson!

Dawson: No I'm not! Everybody knows that basketball is cooler than the swings.

Zion: Who cares about what's cooler? We're just here to have fun!

Dakota: All you care about is being cool, Dawson. You too, Derrick!

Derrick: I can't help it if you just like to do babyish things.

Dawson: Yeah, why don't you go play in the baby playground?

Derrick: Good one, Dawson!

Derrick and Dawson high five each other

Mateo: Hey guys, we're going up the Conflict Escalator. Everybody is getting mad and our amygdalas are taking over.

Tamera: Mateo is right. We need to calm down.

Zion: Yeah that's right. Let's do that Take Five breathing we've been learning.

Derrick, Dawson, and Dakota: Well… okay.

They all do Take Five breathing.

Mateo: Now that we're calm maybe can work out this conflict.

Derrick: Hey, Dakota, I'm sorry I made all the jokes about you being a baby.

Dawson: Yeah, me too. You're not a baby and the swings are fun. I just really felt like playing basketball.

Derrick: Yeah, me too. I'm sorry I got out of control.

Dakota: That's okay guys. We all flip our lids sometimes.

Zion: So what are we going to do?

Tamera: Maybe we should take turns. We could play on the swings today and then play basketball tomorrow.

Mateo: Sounds good to me!

Derrick: Me too! Thanks guys.

Dakota: No problem! Let's go.

Derrick: I bet I can swing the highest!

Dawson: No I can!

Mateo: Not again you guys…. No more conflicts!

Derrick and Dawson: Just kidding!

Everybody laughs. **The End**

Week 27 Skit
The Story I'm Telling Myself

Topic: Fast and slow Thinking

Characters: Julio, Hassan, Tianna, Mom, Narrator 1, Narrator 2

Setting: Outside Tianna's front door and Hassan's house

Narrator 1: Hassan, Tianna and Julio are really good friends. They like to play music together and write their own songs

Narrator 2: One day Hassan went over to Tianna's house and was about to knock on the door when he heard Hassan and Tianna talking.

Narrator 1: He couldn't hear them very well through the door but he listened for a minute. This is what he thought he heard.

Tianna: I think Hassan's new song is really bad.

Julio: Yeah me too.

Hassan: *(Feeling really hurt and mad)* Man that's so mean!

Narrator 2: Hassan turned around and ran home

Later at Hassan's house

Hassan's Mom: Hassan what's wrong? You look really upset

Hassan: Nothing. I'm just mad because of something that happened this afternoon.

Mom: What happened?

Hassan: Well, I heard Tianna tell Julio that my new song really is really bad.

Mom: Really? That doesn't sound like Tianna….

Hassan: Well it is. She's really mean. I don't think I want to be friends with her anymore.

Mom: Wow that's pretty extreme. Don't you think you should talk to her about it?

Hassan: No. She obviously doesn't like any of my songs and has been lying to me this whole time. She's a liar. And Julio said he "totally agrees". What a jerk.

Mom: Really? You've known Tianna and Julio for a long time. They always seem like really good friends.

Hassan: Well, they're not.

Mom: Huh. Well I still think you should talk to them. (walks away)

Narrator 2: The next day:

Narrator 1: Julio and Tianna come over to Hassan's house to pick him up to go to school.

Julio: Hey Hassan!

Hassan:

Tianna: Good morning Hassan!

Hassan:

Tianna: Hassan, I said Good morning. What's up?

Hassan: Nothing.

Julio: Okay…. hey, Tianna and I are thinking we should try out for the school talent show.

Tianna: Yeah.

Hassan: Uh, no thanks. I'm not interested.

Tianna: What? We've been talking about this for weeks…

Julio: Yeah - we can do my new song.

Tianna: No, we should do Hassan's new song.

Hassan: What? **My** new song?!

Tianna: Yeah - it's really good!

Hassan: You're lying. Yesterday I heard you tell Julio that you thought it was really bad!

Tianna: What?! I did not! I said that your new song was really "rad"! It's great!

Hassan: Wait I'm really confused. I totally thought you said it was bad.

Tianna: Why would I say that? That's really mean.

Julio: Geez Hassan - we wouldn't say that.

Hassan: Wow. I had that totally wrong. I just reacted to what I thought I heard and didn't stop to think about it at all. I'm really sorry you guys.

Tianna: No problem!

Julio: Let's go practice your new song!

Hassan: Awesome!

The End

Week 30 Skit
Who's Moving In?

Topic: Gender Stereotypes

Characters: Teddy, Keiko, Joshua, Sophia, Mr. and Ms. Lopez, Indigo, Narrator 1 and Narrator 2

Setting: Four kids are watching their new neighbors move into their apartment building. They're trying to decide what the new kid is going to be like based on the stuff the parents are carrying in.

Narrator 1: Four kids are watching new neighbors move into their apartment building

Teddy: Hey it looks like the new neighbors are moving in!

Keiko: What apartment are they in?

Sophia: 3B - one floor down from me.

Joshua: Do you think they have kids?

Teddy: I don't know.

Mr. Lopez: Hi kids! Do you live in this building?

Sophie: Yeah. Welcome to the neighborhood!

Ms. Lopez: Thanks!

Teddy: Do you have any kids?

Mr. Lopez: Yes! Indigo will be here soon.

Ms. Lopez: Okay back to work.

Narrator 2: Mr. and Ms. Lopez begin carrying in a bunch of stuff belonging to Indigo.

Sophie: Indigo…. Do you think that's a boy or a girl?

Teddy: I don't know….

Keiko: I bet we can tell from their stuff….

Narrator 1: Mr. Lopez walks by carrying an easel.

Teddy: Okay so an artist - so obviously Indigo is a girl.

Keiko: Yeah definitely.

Sophie: But you guys that's ridiculous - haven't you ever heard of Picasso or Leonardo Da Vinci? They were great artists who were men.

Narrator 2: Ms. Lopez walk by carrying a drum set.

Teddy: A drum set, well then Indigo is clearly a boy.

Keiko: Yeah, girls DON'T play the drums.

Joshua: But you guys, that's silly. Girls play all kinds of instruments.

Narrator 1: Mr. Lopez walks by with a soccer ball and a hockey stick.

Teddy: See! Indigo is obviously a boy. He's an athlete!

Sophie: Are you kidding me? Have you heard of the US women's soccer team? They won the world cup like four times in a row!

Narrator 2: Ms. Lopez walks by carrying a globe.

Keiko: Well see obviously she's really smart.

Teddy: But maybe a geek….

Sophie: Hey! I have a globe in <u>my</u> room….

Joshua: Well… (laughing)

Narrator 1: Mr. Lopez walks by carrying a skateboard.

Teddy: Well obviously HE's really cool!

Keiko: Yeah!

Sophia: Uh, you mean SHE's really cool?

Joshua: [high fives her]

Narrator 2: Ms. Lopez walks by with a football jersey.

Teddy: See, I told you! <u>HE</u> loves football.

Narrator 1: Mr. Lopez walks by with pink soccer cleats.

Keiko: Wait….

Teddy: Pink soccer cleats?

Joshua: I have pink soccer cleats - they're awesome! Just like me!

Sophia: I have black ones.

Narrator 2: Ms. Lopez walks by carrying a unicycle.

Teddy: uhhhhhh….

Keiko: hmmmmm….

Sophia and Joshua scratch their heads

Joshua: Now I'm really confused!

Narrator 1: A car pulls up and a kid gets out.

Ms. Lopez: Indigo!

Indigo: Hi Mom!

Mr. Lopez: Indigo, these are our new neighbors.

Indigo: Hey guys!

Teddy: Hi! You have a lot of cool stuff!

Keiko: Yeah, I think we have a lot in common!

Joshua: You play soccer?

Indigo: Yup!

Sophia: Want to go to the park with us and play?

Indigo: Sure! See ya Mom and Dad!

Mr. and Ms. Lopez: Bye kids!

Narrators: The end

Week 31 Skit
"Dude": Standing Up for Others

NOTE: If it makes more sense to substitute another word for "Dude" that is more relevant to your students, please do.

Topic: Standing up against bullying

Characters: 6 kids: Richard, Benson, Aniyah, Andrew, Kidus and Emmanuel

Setting: A park or the playground at recess

Richard: Hey, you guys, let's make some teams for basketball!

Benson: Yeah. I'll be a captain.

Aniyah: I'll be one too.

Andrew: Why do we need captains? Why don't we just count off?

Kidus: Yeah, it's more fun that way.

Emmanuel: Because I only want <u>good</u> people on my team.

Aniyah: Yeah, me too!

Kidus: Well that's not cool, I mean shouldn't everybody get to play?

Emmanuel: Yeah, it's just for fun, it's not like the basketball team or something.

Benson: Oh come on! I only want people who can really play on my team. Like, I don't want to end up with Emmanuel on my team; he shoots like a girl! Am I right?!

Benson laughs and looks around at everyone, but nobody laughs.

Emmanuel looks embarrassed and sad and the other kids look angry.

Aniyah: (Angrily) Dude!

Andrew: (Surprised) Dude!

Kidus: (Angrily) Dude!

Richard: (Calmly) Dude! Don't talk like that. That's offensive and mean.

Everybody except Benson nods in agreement

Andrew: Yeah. And I think that at recess, anybody who wants to play should get to play. When we're on teams, it's different.

Aniyah: I guess you're right. I mean it's fun to play with other kids who are good, but leaving kids out just because they aren't as good yet seems kind of mean.

Richard: I heard that there used to be a kid at this school who used a wheelchair.

Benson: Really?

Richard: Yeah, but the other kids didn't want him to be left out of everything so they found ways to include him in their games.

Aniyah: That's cool.

Emmanuel: I have asthma which makes it hard for me to breathe sometimes when I run around. I'm not really able to run fast enough to be on a team, but I still really like playing basketball. Recess is my only chance.

Benson: I never really thought of it like that.

Aniyah: Dude, I'll show you how girls shoot (pretends to shoot and swish!).

Richard: Whoa! Swish!

Kidus: That's right! (high fives Aniyah)

Benson: All right, you guys, I'm sorry. Come on, let's go play. We'll count off for teams.

Everybody (Happily) Dude!! (high fives all around)

The End.

Worksheets and Posters

In this section you will find reproducible Worksheets for your class.

Worksheets

Week 1	Who is my Kindness Pal?
Week 2	My Kindness Pal's Favorite Things
Week 3	Same and Different
Week 4	See, Hear, Feel
Week 6	Find Your Feelings
Week 21	Apology Practice 1 and 2
Week 22	Toolbox Matching Game
Week 26	Remote Control Breathing
Week 30	Gender Stereotypes

Week 1
Who is my Kindness Pal?

Your Name _____

Here are some things I know about my new pal:

_____
_____
_____
_____
_____
_____
_____
_____
_____

Here are some kind acts I could do for my pal:

✔ Stack their chair
✔ Get their backpack
✔ Draw them a picture
✔ Give them a compliment
✔ Play with them at recess
✔ Sit with them at lunch
✔ Give them a small gift

✔ _____
✔ _____
✔ _____
✔ _____
✔ _____
✔ _____

Week 2
My Kindness Pal's Favorite Things

Your Name _____

My Pal's favorite movie: _____

My Pal's favorite book: _____

My Pal's favorite place to visit: _____

What my Pal likes MOST about school: _____

What my Pal likes LEAST about school: _____

My Pal's favorite food: _____

My Pal's favorite singer/musician: _____

My Pal doesn't like it when people: _____

My Pal loves it when people: _____

When my Pal grows up they would like to be: _____

My Pal wishes the world were more: _____

My Pal is worried about: _____

The person/s my Pal admires the most is: _____

If my Pal could meet anyone it would be: _____

My Pal always laughs when: _____

One word to describe my Pal is: _____

Week 3
Same and Different 1

Your Name _____

My Pal and are the same on the inside because:

_____
_____
_____

_____
_____
_____

My Pal and I are different on the inside because:

_____
_____
_____

_____
_____
_____

Week 3
Same and Different 2

Your Name _____

My Pal and are the *same* **on the outside because:**

_____
_____
_____
_____

_____
_____

My Pal and I are *different* **on the outside because:**

_____
_____
_____
_____

_____
_____

Week 4
See, Hear, Feel

Your Name _____

What did you see, hear, feel?

See:

_____
_____
_____
_____
_____

Feel:

_____
_____
_____
_____
_____

Hear:

_____
_____
_____
_____
_____

Week 6
Find Your Feelings

Your Name _____

Where do you feel your emotions in your body?

Calm	Happy
Scared	Sad
Grouchy	Nervous
Cheerful	Excited
Confident	Relaxed
Shy	Silly
Proud	Embarrassed
Miserable	Terrified
Jubilant	Discouraged
Enraged	Panicky
Ecstatic	Confused

Week 21
Apology Practice Worksheet 1

Your Name _____

Mean it – Own it – Fix it – Let it go
Analyze each apology and choose the best one.

Someone knocks over your magnetic tile tower. They say: "Sorry! I was in a hurry to get in line."

Mean it _____
Own it _____
Fix it _____
Let it go _____

Someone knocks over your magnetic tile tower. They say: "Sorry! Your tower is too tall. It was about to fall over anyway."

Mean it _____
Own it _____
Fix it _____
Let it go _____

Someone knocks over your magnetic tile tower. They say: "Oh no! I'm sorry I knocked over your tower! Can I help you build it again?"

Mean it _____
Own it _____
Fix it _____
Let it go _____

Someone knocks over your magnetic tile tower. They say: "Oh no! I'm sorry! Can I help you build it again?" You say "That's okay. I'll just clean up the tiles." They say, "But I said I'm sorry! You have to accept my apology! Let me help you build it!"

Mean it _____
Own it _____
Fix it _____
Let it go _____

Week 21
Apology Practice Worksheet 2

Your Name _____

Mean it – Own it – Fix it – Let it go
Analyze each apology and choose the best one.

You are hurrying to line up for recess and you accidentally trip somebody and they fall down. They say, "Hey! You tripped me!" You say, "Sorry!"

Mean it _____
Own it _____
Fix it_____
Let it go _____

You are hurrying to line up for recess and you accidentally trip somebody and they fall down. They say, "Hey! You tripped me!" You say, "Oh sorry you fell. I was in a hurry."

Mean it _____
Own it _____
Fix it_____
Let it go _____

You are hurrying to line up for recess and you accidentally trip somebody and they fall down. They say, "Hey! You tripped me!" You say, "Oh I'm so sorry!! I was rushing and I wasn't watching where I was going. I'm really sorry. Are you okay? Do you want to get in front of me?"

Mean it _____
Own it _____
Fix it_____
Let it go _____

You are hurrying to line up for recess and you accidentally trip somebody and they fall down. They say, "Hey! You tripped me!" You say, "Oh I'm so sorry!! I was rushing and I wasn't watching where I was going. I'm really sorry. Are you okay? Do you want to get in front of me?" They say, "No that's okay." They still look upset. You say, "Come on, I said I was sorry!!! Why are you still mad at me? It was just an accident. Geez."

Mean it _____
Own it _____
Fix it_____
Let it go _____

Week 22
Toolbox Matching Game

Your Name _____

Share

Take Turns

Get Help

Leave it to Chance

Pause the Conflict

Be Kind

Compromise

Skip the Conflict

Week 26
Remote Control Breathing

Your Name _____

Did your mind change the channel during your mindfulness practice?
List some of the channels that you noticed:

_____
_____
_____
_____
_____
_____
_____
_____
_____
_____
_____
_____

Week 30
Gender Stereotypes

Look at the items on this list and discuss with your partner whether you associate them with boys or girls. Talk about why you feel that way.

1. Art supplies _____
2. Drum set _____
3. Soccer ball _____
4. Hockey stick _____
5. Globe _____
6. Skateboard _____
7. Football jersey _____
8. Pink soccer cleats _____
9. Unicycle _____
10. Chef hat _____
11. Microscope _____
12. Broom _____
13. Baseball glove _____
14. Book _____
15. Laundry basket _____
16. Cell phone _____
17. Snow shovel _____
18. Violin _____
19. Knitting needles _____
20. Chess set _____

Diagram of Three Parts of the Brain

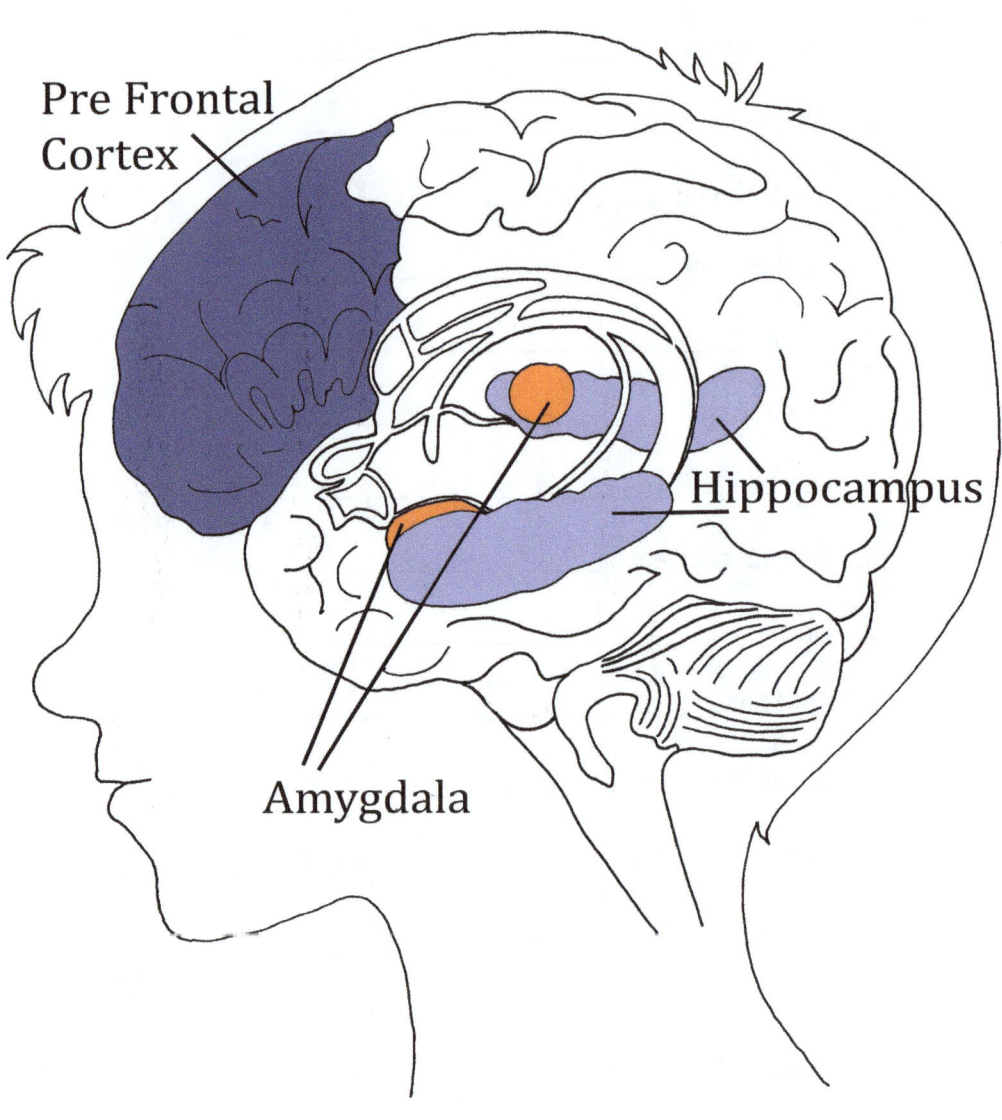

The Conflict Toolbox

1. SHARE
2. TAKE TURNS
3. BE KIND
4. LEAVE IT TO CHANCE
5. COMPROMISE
6. PAUSE THE CONFLICT
7. SKIP THE CONFLICT
8. GET HELP

The Conflict CAT

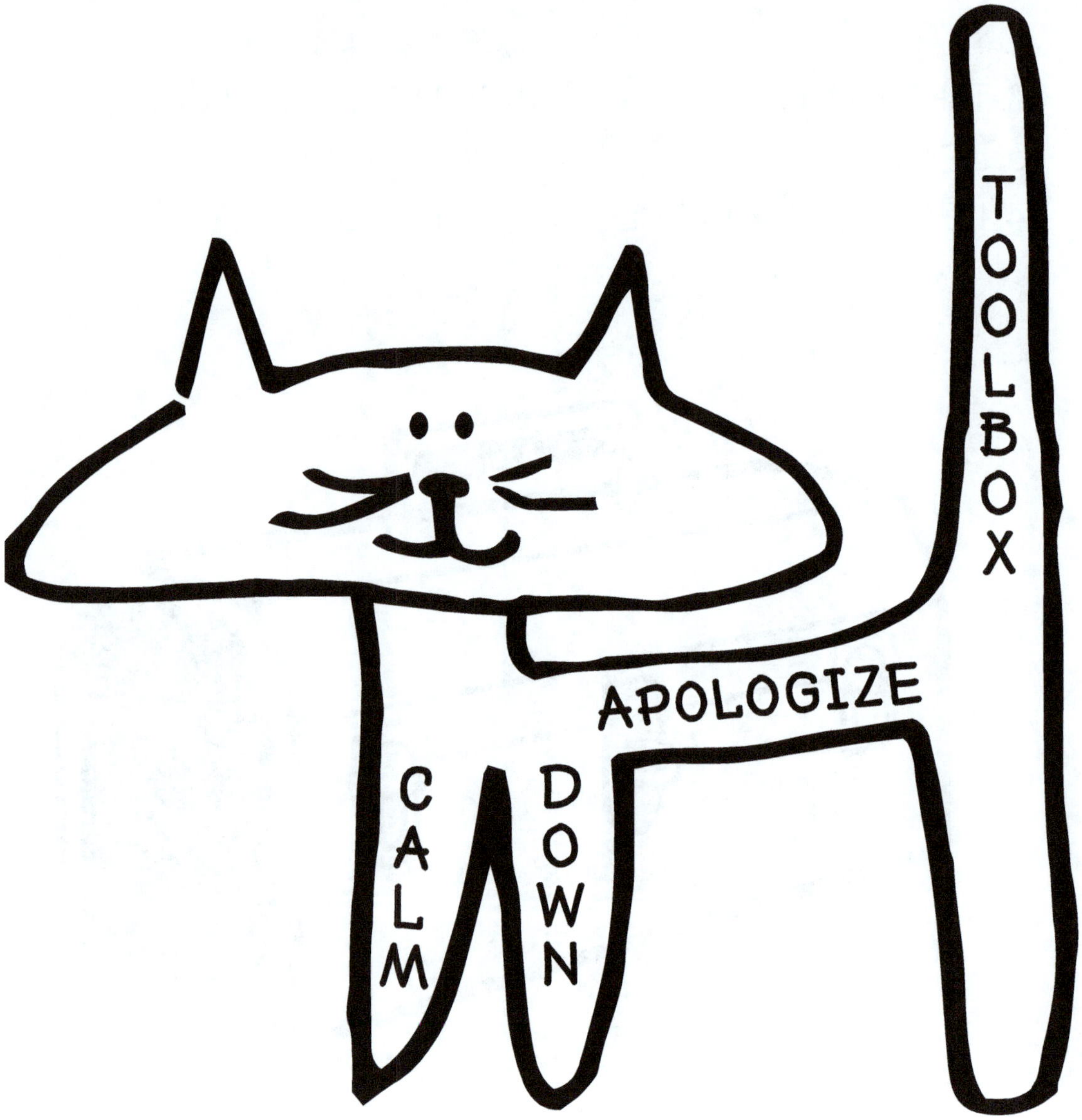

Kindness Pals List

for the week of _____

Student	Student
1.	
2.	
3.	
4.	
5.	
6.	
7.	
8.	
9.	
10.	
11.	
12.	
13.	
14.	
15.	

The Conflict Escalator

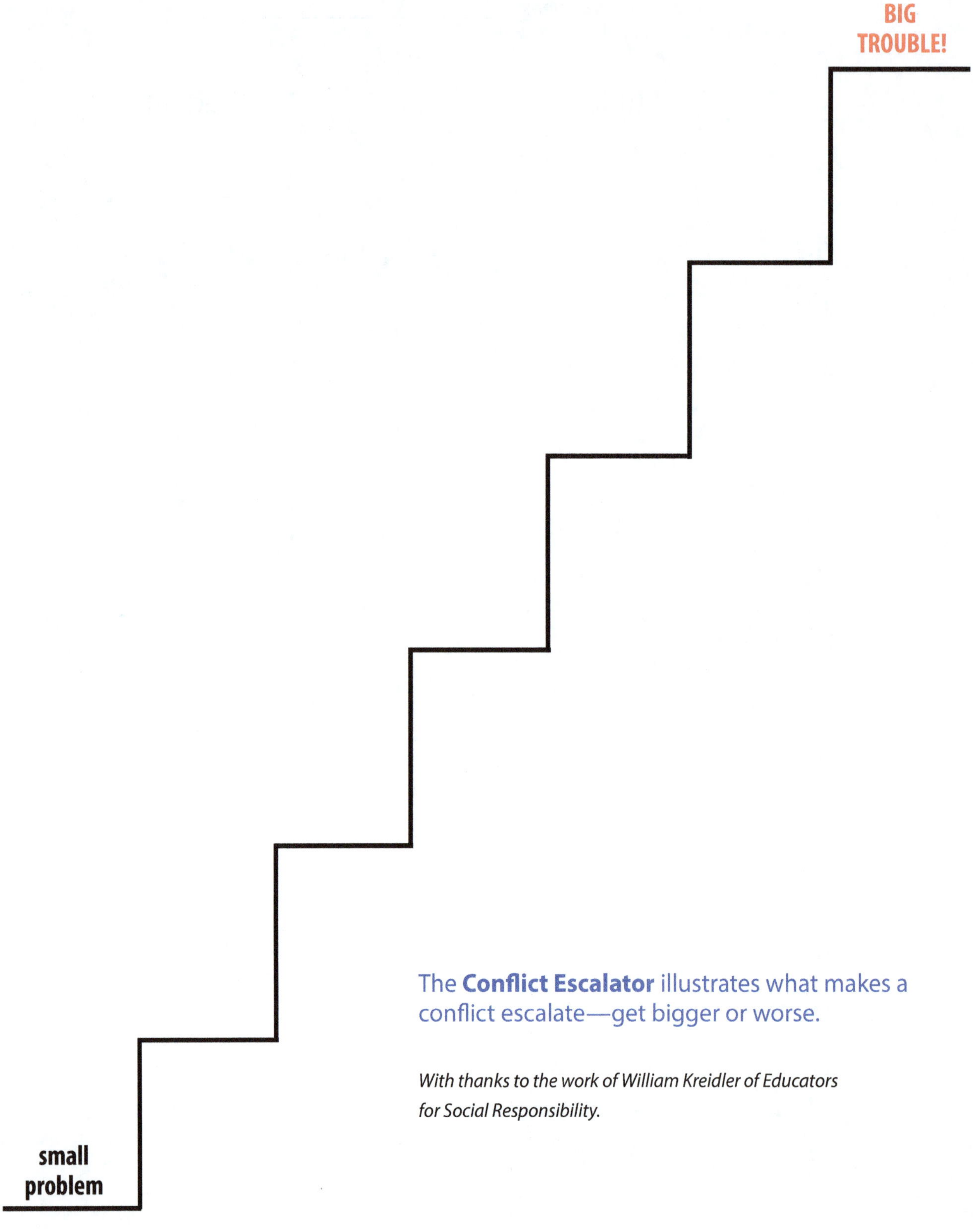

BIG TROUBLE!

The **Conflict Escalator** illustrates what makes a conflict escalate—get bigger or worse.

With thanks to the work of William Kreidler of Educators for Social Responsibility.

small problem

Books, Videos and Games

Books Used In Lessons

- *Weird!: A Story About Dealing with Bullying in Schools* (The Weird! Series) by Erin Frankel and illustrated by Paula Heaphy
- *Dare!* (The Weird! Series) by Erin Frankel and illustrated by Paula Heaphy
- *Tough!: A Story about How to Stop Bullying in Schools* (The Weird! Series) by Erin Frankel and illustrated by Paula Heaphy
- *Rosie's Brain* by Linda Ryden; illustrated by Shearry Malone
- *Sergio Sees the Good* by Linda Ryden; illustrated by Shearry Malone
- *Tyaja Uses the THiNK Test* by Linda Ryden, illustrated by Shearry Malone

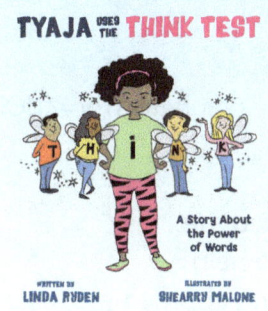

Videos and Games Used In Lessons

Week 1   Take Five Breathing
https://TeachPeaceofMind.org/students-2/

Week 3   Four Square Breathing
https://TeachPeaceofMind.org/students-2/

Gravity Hands
https://TeachPeaceofMind.org/students-2/

Clench and Release
http://www.yomind.com/justme

Week 9   Head Shoulders Knees & Toes
https://TeachPeaceofMind.org/students-2/

Week 18   Hand Model of Brain
https://www.youtube.com/watch?v=f-m2YcdMdFw

Week 29   Run Like a Girl
https://www.youtube.com/watch?v=XjJQBjWYDTs

The Conflict CAT Game

Peace of Mind created the Conflict CAT Game to help students integrate and apply skills they have been learning, including mindfulness practice, apologizing, and using tools to resolve conflicts. This game is optional - but very helpful and fun! Available at TeachPeaceofMind.org.

VII. Resources

Comprehensive Whole School Integration

Consider moving the lessons of **Peace of Mind** beyond the classroom with one or more of these Program extensions. Each offers opportunities for students to hone their new mindfulness skills, to practice kindness, develop as leaders, and to use the common language and tools they are learning to resolve conflicts.

Daily Mindful Moments

The **Peace of Mind** Curriculum is designed to be taught as a weekly class. If you have the time and desire to make **Peace of Mind** a part of your classroom every day, that's wonderful! Daily Mindful Moments are a great way for your students to practice the skills that they are learning weekly in **Peace of Mind** class and to enjoy a moment of calm and quiet before beginning a new activity. It just takes a couple of minutes. Once you get into the habit it will be something that is beneficial to both you and your students.

You may want to make "Mindfulness Helper" a weekly job in your classroom and have that student lead the Daily Mindful Moment. You may decide to lead the Daily Mindful Moment yourself at the beginning to set the tone and expectations and then transition to a student-led practice. Either way is fine. You can also experiment with the duration of the quiet moment. Some classes will have no problem with two minutes and will quickly graduate to more; some classes will be better off with one minute or less to start.

Mindful Mentors

Mindful Mentors is a leadership program you may want to institute for fifth graders. Mindful Mentors visit younger grade classrooms once or twice a week to lead a Mindful Moment.

The mentors grow from having the opportunity to be leaders in the school, and leading mindfulness practice helps them build confidence and ease in using practices themselves. The younger kids are inspired to do the mindfulness practices because they look up to the fifth graders.

Give it a try!

Peace Club

Peace Club is a lunch and recess program for students who need a smaller alternative to the cafeteria and the playground. It can be a mixed-age group of anywhere from 20-50 students. Peace Club requires all students who come to make a promise to treat everyone else with kindness and respect and to make sure that conflicts are worked out peacefully and everyone is included.

Peace Club is meant to be a comfortable option for kids who sometimes struggle with their social skills or with being in a large group. It is also popular among kids who like to make a difference and who make a commitment to making everyone feel welcome and respected. At Lafayette Elementary School, for example, children on the autism spectrum and with other diagnoses often have Peace Club specifically written into their IEP's and 504 plans because Peace Club provides some structured play as well as informal group counseling during the hour.

Fourth and fifth graders might serve as special helpers. These are kids who make an extra commitment to seek out those who have a harder time jumping in and include them in games, and who help others work out conflicts peacefully.

Linkages to Behavior Management Programs

Peace of Mind is different from other Mindfulness or SEL curricula in that *Peace of Mind* teaches mindfulness as the essential foundation for students' acquisition and practice of social and emotional skills, including conflict resolution.

The goal of **Peace of Mind** is to help students develop the internal motivation to use skills they have learned to make mindful choices to govern their actions, speech and movement, motivated by kindness and empathy, and shored up by an understanding of their brains. **Peace of Mind**, and especially the mindfulness skills it teaches, can be a powerful support to increase the impact of externally motivated behavior modification programs.

For example, Lafayette Elementary School in Washington D.C. turned their Positive Behavioral Intervention and Supports (PBIS) program into a mindfulness-based program that combines intrinsic and extrinsic motivation. Rather than relying solely on a list of school rules and external rewards to regulate students' behavior, the school developed a set of guidelines based in mindfulness: Speak Mindfully, Act Mindfully, and Move Mindfully, or "SAMM".

Children are encouraged to notice where they are in the building - the library, the gym, the cafeteria - and then to ask themselves: How loudly can I talk? How quickly can I move? Students are asked to think about how they treat other people in every situation, and to ask: could I be kind to the new student sitting alone? Could I help the child who just dropped their pencil box? This way they begin to be mindfully aware of what is happening around them and to make choices about how to behave accordingly in that moment.

Asking students to use mindfulness skills to take responsibility for their actions is very empowering and can result in a significant difference in student self-regulation and school climate.

Home-School Connection

A September 2018 national study by Learning Heroes, *Developing Life Skills in Children: A Road Map for Communicating with Parents*, showed that 8 in 10 parents believe teaching and reinforcing social and emotional learning skills in school is very important.

Parents and guardians would like to count on schools as partners in teaching "life skills" to their children, and would like to be informed about what is being taught in Peace of Mind Class. We know from experience and from the Learning Heroes study that the two informants they trust most are their children and their children's teacher.

News from their children
Encourage your students to share what they have learned at home with trusted adults. You will notice that many lesson extensions in this curriculum encourage children to share what they are learning with family members. Provide time in class to allow students to reflect on this sharing.

Newsletter
Sending home a weekly or monthly newsletter with updates on what you are teaching in **Peace of Mind** Class is very helpful. Parents and guardians appreciate knowing about the themes of the lessons you are teaching, and also the names of practices, such as Take Five Breathing, that they can ask their children to demonstrate for them at home.

Back to School Night
We've found offering parents information about **Peace of Mind** at Back to School Night is very helpful. Please see the **Peace of Mind** website (TeachPeaceofMind.org) for materials that may be helpful to you in explaining the program. Photos and videos of your students practicing

mindfulness can also be powerful tools to help parents understand what their children are learning.

Parent Evenings

Parents may be interested in an evening event in which they can experience some of the lessons and skills their children are learning. Introducing parents to the language of the curriculum can be helpful, too. Having a common language allows parents to prompt their children to use the skills they are learning at home.

You can find additional resources for parents on the **Peace of Mind** website at **TeachPeaceofMind.org.**

Teacher Support

Resources to Support your Teaching

Daniel Siegel's Brain Talk Video (YouTube) http://www.drdansiegel.com/resources/everyday_mindsight_tools/

Breeding, K., & Harrison, J. (2007). *Connected and Respected: Lessons from the Resolving Conflict Creatively Program.* Cambridge, Mass.: Educators for Social Responsibility.

Jennings, P. (2015). *Mindfulness for teachers: Simple skills for peace and productivity in the classroom.* The Norton Series on the Social Neuroscience of Education.

Jennings, P. A. (2019). *The Trauma-Sensitive Classroom: Building Resilience with Compassionate Teaching.* New York: W.W. Norton & Company.

Rechtschaffen, D., & Kabat-Zinn PhD, J. (2014). *The Way of Mindful Education: Cultivating Well-being in Teachers and Students.* Norton Books in Education.

Simmons, Dena (2019), *Why We Can't Afford Whitewashed Social and Emotional Learning* ASCD.org.

Srinivasan, M. (2014). *Teach, Breathe, Learn: Mindfulness in and out of the Classroom.* Berkeley, CA: Parallax Press.

TED. (2014, December 15). Verna Myers: *How to overcome our biases? Walk boldly toward them.* Retrieved from https://www.youtube.com/watch?v=uYyvbgINZkQ

Treleaven, David (2018). *Trauma-Sensitive Mindfulness: Practices for Safe and Transformative Healing.* New York: W. W. Norton & Company.

Collaborative for Academic Social and Emotional Learning. https://Casel.org

Center for the Greater Good at U.C. Berkeley https://greatergood.berkeley.edu/

Center for Healthy Minds at the U. of Wisconsin https://centerhealthyminds.org/

Mindful Schools Resource Pages http://www.mindfulschools.org/

Mindfulness, Bias and Equity https://www.mindfulpowertobe.com/

Resources for Personal Mindfulness Practice and Well-being

Apps to Get You Started

Ten Percent Happier App
Headspace
Calm

Good reads about developing a secular mindfulness practice

Ten Percent Happier and *Meditation for Fidgety Skeptics* by Dan Harris and Jeff Warren

The Mindful Athlete by George Mumford

Hardwiring Happiness by Dr. Rick Hanson

Say What You Mean: A Mindful Approach to Nonviolent Communication by Oren Jay Sofer

Online Mindfulness Courses

Mindful Schools Courses for Educators	https://www.mindfulschools.org/
Elements of Meditation with Jeff Warren courses/	https://jeffwarren.THiNKific.com/
Unified Mindfulness	https://unifiedmindfulness.com

A few of the many wonderful Mindfulness Teachers out there to help you develop your practice (online or in person)

Sharon Salzberg
Real Love

https://www.sharonsalzberg.com

George Mumford
Mindfulness for Performance

https://georgemumford.com/

Grace Helms Kotre
Mindfulness, Bias, Equity

https://www.mindfulpowertobe.com/

Sebene Selassie
Belonging and Identity

https://www.sebeneselassie.com

VIII. Bibliography

Bradshaw, C. P. (2015). Translating research to practice in bullying prevention. American Psychologist, 70 (4), 322-332.

Breeding, K., & Harrison, J. (2007). *Connected and Respected: Lessons from the Resolving Conflict Creatively Program.* Cambridge, Mass.: Educators for Social Responsibility.

Durlak, J. A., Weissberg, R. P., Dymnicki, A. B., Taylor, R. D. & Schellinger, K. B. (2011). The impact of enhancing students' social and emotional learning: A meta-analysis of school-based universal interventions. Child Development, 82(1): 405–432.

Hanson, R. (2015). *Hardwiring Happiness*. Random House USA.

Jennings, P. (2015). *Mindfulness for teachers: Simple skills for peace and productivity in the classroom.* The Norton Series on the Social Neuroscience of Education.

Jennings, P. A. (2019). *The Trauma-Sensitive Classroom: Building Resilience with Compassionate Teaching.* New York: W.W. Norton & Company.

Kahneman, D. (2015). *Thinking, Fast and Slow*. New York: Farrar, Straus and Giroux.

Lantieri, Linda. "How SEL and Mindfulness Can Work Together." Greater Good. April 7, 2015. Accessed September 28, 2015. http://greatergood.berkeley.edu/article/item/how_social_emotional_learning_and_mindfulness_can_work_together.

Learning Heroes, *Developing Life Skills in Children: A Road Map for Communicating with Parents*, https://bealearninghero.org/parent-mindsets/ September 2018

Metz, S.M., Frank, J.L., Reibel, D., Cantrell, T., Sanders, R., & Broderick, P.C. (2013). The effectiveness of Learning to BREATHE program on adolescent emotion regulation. *Research in Human Development, 10*(3), 252-272.

O'Brennan, L., & Bradshaw, C. (2013). School Climate: A Research Brief. A report prepared for the National Education Association, Washington, DC.

Rechtschaffen, D., & Kabat-Zinn PhD, J. (2014). *The Way of Mindful Education: Cultivating Well-being in Teachers and Students.* Norton Books in Education.

Schonert-Reichl, K. A., & Lawlor, M. S. (2010). The effects of a mindfulness-based education program on pre-and early adolescents' well-being and social and emotional competence. *Mindfulness, 1*(3), 137-151.

Schonert-Reichl, K. A., Oberle, E., Lawlor, M. S., Abbott, D., Thomson, K., Oberlander, T. F., & Diamond, A. (2015). Enhancing cognitive and social–emotional development through a simple-to-administer mindfulness-based school program for elementary school children: A randomized controlled trial. *Developmental Psychology, 51*(1), 52-66.

Seppala, E., Simon-Thomas, E., Brown, S. L., Worline, M. C., Cameron, C. D., & Doty, J. R. (2017). *The Oxford Handbook of Compassion Science.* New York, NY: Oxford University Press.

Siegel, D. J., & Bryson, T. P. (2012). *The Whole-Brain Child.* London: Constable & Robinson.

Simmons, Dena (2019), *Why We Can't Afford Whitewashed Social-Emotional Learning* Retrieved from http://www.ascd.org/publications/newsletters/education_update/apr19/vol61/num04

Srinivasan, M. (2014). *Teach, Breathe, Learn: Mindfulness in and out of the Classroom.* Berkeley, CA: Parallax Press.

Treleaven, David (2018). *Trauma-Sensitive Mindfulness: Practices for Safe and Transformative Healing.* New York: W. W. Norton & Company.

Weare, K. (2013). Developing mindfulness with children and young people: A review of the evidence and policy context. *Journal of Children's Services, 8(*2), 141-153.

Zoogman, S., Goldberg, S.B., Hoyt, W.T., & Miller, L. (2015). Mindfulness interventions with youth: A meta-analysis. *Mindfulness, 6*, 290 - 302.

Zenner, C., Hermleben-Kurz, S., & Walach, H. (2014). Mindfulness-based interventions in schools: A systematic review and meta-analysis. *Frontiers in Psychology, 5*, article 603.

IX. Credits

Hand Model of the Brain: Dr. Dan Siegel's *Hand Model of the Brain*. Found at https://www.youtube.com/watch?v=f-m2YcdMdFw. 2017 Mind Your Brain, Inc. Used with permission. All rights reserved.

"See, Hear, Feel": Shinzen Young, Unified Mindfulness. Unifiedmindfulness.com

The Conflict Escalator: Kreidler, William J., *Teaching Conflict Resolution through Children's Literature*. New York: Scholastic Professional Books, 1994

The THiNK Test: TOP 16 QUOTES BY BERNARD MELTZER: A-Z Quotes. (n.d.). Retrieved from https://www.azquotes.com/author/9957-Bernard_Meltzer

Children's Photos: Stacy Beck Photography and LNJ Designs Photo

Drawings: Linda Ryden

X. Appreciation

Linda's students have been our greatest teachers, our inspiration, and our joy. Each one of the more than 1,000 children Linda has worked with at Lafayette Elementary School in Washington, D.C. has taught us something important, and some have left lasting imprints on our hearts. These children, some of who are in college now, fill us with hope that they will create a more peaceful world than the one they were born into.

We owe a huge debt of gratitude to the wonderful teachers at Peace of Mind's home school, Lafayette Elementary, and all of our DCPS Pilot Schools who have welcomed and supported the **Peace of Mind** Program. Leaders Liz Whisnant, Megan Vroman and Jordan Love, especially, have gone above and beyond. Special thanks to Jared Catapano for taking up the challenge and becoming both a mindfulness teacher and, more importantly, a mindful teacher.

Lafayette's amazing School Counselor Jillian Diesner took on the challenge of adapting the **Peace of Mind** curriculum to our youngest students and has contributed so much of her expertise and creativity to expand **Peace of Mind** in wonderful new ways.

In this testing-focused culture it takes courage to set aside time in the school day for something that can't be easily quantified. Many thanks to Lafayette Principal Dr. Carrie Broquard for her enthusiastic support for the **Peace of Mind** program. Thanks to her leadership and willingness to go out on a limb, **Peace of Mind** has grown into an effective model program.

Peace of Mind would not have been possible without the generous financial support of the Lafayette Home and School Association. Many thanks to all members, past and present, for supporting the program over the years, and for making our children's social emotional development a priority.

We are grateful to the many people whose work inspires and informs the **Peace of Mind Program.** Thank you to Annie Mahon for planting the very early seeds of the Peace program at Lafayette and for continuing to shine the light on Mindfulness. From the very beginning Colman McCarthy, journalist and peace teacher, inspired us to find a way to teach peace. So much of what is offered in these pages is inspired by the work of these wonderful teachers: Dan Harris, Jeff Warren, Rick Hanson, Sharon Salzberg, Oren Jay Sofer, Jay Michelson, and Sebene Selassie.

Our nonprofit organization, Peace of Mind Inc, is guided and sustained by an extraordinary Board of Directors. Enormous thanks to Rie Odsbjerg, Jackie

Snowden, Liz Whisnant, Darrel Jodrey, Chapin Springer and Subrat Biswal for all that you give and have given. Thanks, too, to our Advisors whose input has been invaluable: Avideh Shashaani, JusTme, Harriet Sanford, Dr. Elizabeth Hoffman, Dave Trachtenberg and Janine Rudder. And finally, a shout-out to all of our wonderful interns, including Madeleine Sagebiel whose positive, skillful help was instrumental in the final stages of getting this curriculum to the publisher. We couldn't do it without you!

With love and gratitude,

Linda   Cheryl.

Linda Ryden and Cheryl Cole Dodwell, August 2019

About Linda Ryden, Teacher and Author

Linda started teaching "Peace Class" in 2003. Since then, her classes have grown into the **Peace of Mind** program which has become an integral part of the school curriculum and climate at Lafayette Elementary School in Washington DC. In 2014 Linda and Cheryl Cole Dodwell published the *Peace of Mind Curriculum* which is now being used in schools across the country and around the world. While still happily working full-time as the Peace Teacher at Lafayette teaching 700 students per week, Linda founded Peace of Mind Inc., a nonprofit organization, to advocate for a Peace Teacher in every school, to share the *Peace of Mind Curriculum*, and to support other educators who are bringing mindfulness- and brain-science based social and emotional learning to their students in the Washington DC area

and nationwide. Linda is the author of four books for children, *Rosie's Brain*, (published by Peace of Mind Press), *Henry is Kind, Sergio Sees the Good*, and *Tyaja Uses the THiNK Test* (published by Tilbury House and illustrated by Shearry Malone). Linda's work has been recognized in the *Washington Post*, the *Huffington Post*, and on CBS, ABC and Fox5 News.

In that small but growing band of peace educators, Linda Ryden stands out. The glistening ideas and stories in these pages are sure to open minds and stir hearts, in much the way that has been happening all these years with the children in her classrooms.

- Colman McCarthy, Founder of The Center for Teaching Peace

About Cheryl Cole Dodwell

Cheryl, the Executive Director of Peace of Mind Inc., is the co-author of the *Peace of Mind Core Curriculum for Grades 1 and 2* and the *Peace of Mind Core Curriculum for Grades 3-5* and oversees the development of the *Peace of Mind Curriculum Series, Henry and Friends Storybook Series* and resources. Cheryl brings dedication and passion, a love of writing and editing, a background in finance, publishing and nonprofit management, and deep experience in mindfulness and healing work to her work with **Peace of Mind**. She is grateful to be able to contribute her time and talents to help make our world a kinder and more supportive place for us all.